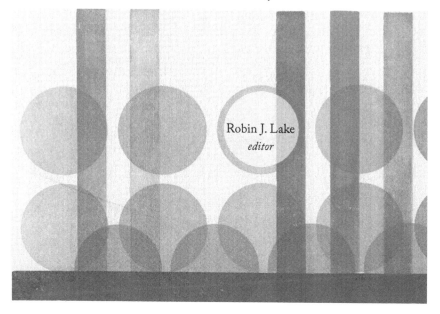

Robin J. Lake
editor

Unique Schools Serving
Unique Students

CHARTER SCHOOLS AND CHILDREN WITH SPECIAL NEEDS

center on reinventing public education

Unique Schools Serving Unique Students: Charter Schools and Children with Special Needs, edited by Robin J. Lake

Design by Kate Basart/Union Pageworks

ISBN: 978-0-615-368115

Center on Reinventing Public Education
National Charter School Research Project
University of Washington
Seattle, Washington
www.crpe.org

The Center on Reinventing Public Education at the University of Washington engages in independent research and policy analysis on a range of K-12 public education reform issues, including choice & charters, finance & productivity, teachers, urban district reform, leadership, and state & federal reform.

The National Charter School Research Project (NCSRP) brings rigor, evidence, and balance to the national charter school debate. NCSRP was established at the Center on Reinventing Public Education in 2004 with support from a consortium of funders.

Contents

Foreword

EUGENE EDGAR

Let me start by acknowledging that I have not been a huge supporter of the charter school concept. However, over the past few years, especially with the advance of charter schools, I have mellowed on my opposition. Reading this collection of essays has helped me become an advocate for public charter schools.

This volume goes a long way toward helping clarify how public charter schools can (and do) serve students with disabilities. Additionally, there is a comprehensive analysis of the legal barriers that charter schools, indeed all schools, face in serving this population. Perhaps this analysis of the legal issues will move the field to consider ways to lift some of the onerous requirements of the law.

There is major disagreement within the field of special education as to the most effective way to deliver education to students in need of special services. The examples of successful charter special education programs in this book will be cheered by some and condemned by others. Those who champion specialized schools for youth with disabilities will be pleased to read about the Metro Deaf School, although others who champion "least restrictive environments" may not be as happy. The ISUS Institute of Construction Technology will be music to the ears of educators concerned about the rush to prepare every student for college, but may put frowns on the faces of those convinced that college attendance is the only satisfactory outcome for all. I would think that few will find fault with the kinds of integrated programs described at the Charyl Stockwell Academy and the CHIME Arnold Schwarzenegger Charter Elementary School.

Although special education law and prevailing thought assume we have the knowledge and technology to accurately assess disabilities, there is considerable strength to the contrary position that the current system is based on faulty notions both about the nature of disability and how best to respond to children and youth with special needs.[1] This alternative viewpoint calls for a radical redefinition of disability and the corresponding response to students so labeled. Thus, any system that perpetuates current definitions is in essence perpetuating the problem. Advocates of this alternative line of thinking will not find much

---

1. Andrews et al., 2000, 258–60, 267.

to celebrate in this volume. What they will find, however, are multiple examples of how charter school personnel have formed learning communities to take on the responsibility of educating all children who enter their buildings. By any standard and wherever one stands on charter schools, this is an encouraging finding for all interested in serving the needs of students with disabilities.

The major finding from the six case studies contained here is that charter schools with five basic characteristics tend to provide strong programs for students with disabilities. These characteristics are schoolwide communities dedicated to serving all students, effective professional support for teachers, customized student interventions, a focus on effective instruction, and safe, respectful student-to-student interactions. Ideally, these features would exist in every school, not simply charter schools serving students with disabilities. These characteristics are strikingly similar to the ideas proposed by John Goodlad and Tom Skrtic.[2] Goodlad and his associates have long advocated for schools to engage in a process of ongoing inquiry (identified as "continuous renewal"), where the building community continuously asks questions about the purpose and outcomes of their work and makes adjustments as needed. This line of thought posits that no outside reform will ever be able to address the needs of specific school buildings. Skrtic proposes that schools become "ad hocracies," where the factory model of education is replaced by learning communities in which roles are shared and created as needed by the current situation. In short, innovation would replace standardization. These characteristics are important for all schools and I would hope this volume can advance the notion of buildings becoming learning communities grounded in the idea that all children, including those with disabilities, are viable members of that community.

Important decisions in life almost always require individuals and societal institutions to make decisions between competing goods: between freedom and constraint, the short term and the long term, the individual and the community. One such tension concerns parental choice in public schooling. Clearly the charter school movement has been built on the notion of the importance of parent choice. In fact, a major finding from this volume is that charter schools provide parents of students with disabilities yet another choice in finding a school that meets their children's needs. And, as noted by this volume, parents of children are "hyper-shoppers" in searching for schools for their children. So, parent choice is a major issue to unpack.

Who can possibly question the inherent goodness of parent choice in selecting schools for their children, especially the parents of children with disabilities? Choice falls into the category of life tensions, specifically around the idea of choice for individual (or family) advancement versus the common good. As

---

2. Goodlad, 1984; Tom Skrtic, 1991, 148–206.

individuals make choices, they influence the life chances of their immediate family and the welfare of the entire community. Parents who choose schools for their children based on finding the "best school" to advance their child are making choices that advance the good of the individual (family), perhaps over the good of the community as a whole. One cannot "blame" parents for making this choice, especially parents of children with disabilities, but the question remains, who is responsible for thinking about the common good?

The public schools, at least the P–12 public schools, are the major institution of democratic societies where people from all societal backgrounds can come together in a common space to learn to negotiate conjoint living. If choice were evenly distributed across all families, then choice for individual advancement versus the common good might be mitigated, but we know choice is not evenly distributed across the population of parents searching for schools. In fact, social class rears its ugly head at this point. Parents with resources tend to take advantage of choice more so than families that are economically poor. Given this reality, parent choice contributes to the separation of citizens by class. Of course, there are other factors that account for this separation (housing patterns, job distribution, access to higher education, and more), but when any process results in segregation by class (or race, gender, ability, or any other demographic status), the public purpose of public schools is endangered.

One might consider choice to be congregation rather than separation, that is to say, a situation in which people make choices to be together as opposed to putting up barriers to others joining them. However, I would argue that, left unfettered, parent choice plays a significant factor in segregating children from economically poor families. Now I deeply wish that the common schools were so uncommonly good that the vast majority of parents would choose local neighborhood schools. Until that hope is realized, I think we need to work hard to decrease the segregation of children in our public schools. Charter schools, because of their core idea of parent choice, must step up to the possibility of increased segregation by economic status and develop policy and procedures that will mitigate this potential problem.

Who is responsible for preventing segregation? I would argue that it is unreasonable to place that burden on parents (especially parents with children with disabilities). Still, who should carry this load? It is easy for individual actors within the system—teachers, principals, developers of charter schools, individual public officials, and university leaders—to disclaim the responsibility of being the gatekeepers to public education. But just as easily, each group, including the parents, could take on the role of gatekeeper.

Walter Parker has explored this issue in depth.[3] In an article entitled "Teaching Against Idiocy," Parker presents the dilemma of choice when families make choices that maximize their material, short-term advantage while assuming that all others will do likewise. Parker identifies this as idiotic behavior—idiotic in the sense of childish, as opposed to more mature civic behavior. His major hope for addressing this issue and creating citizens that are concerned with the common good are public schools that hold close to their heart the notion that schools have the responsibility for developing citizens.

Charter schools can and do play a crucial role in the debate as to the purpose of public schooling. While there are contested sides to this argument, I take the position that public schools in a democracy have three equal major purposes: (1) to provide individual students with the knowledge, skills, and dispositions that enhance their individual pursuit of life, liberty, and happiness; (2) to provide those benefits to all students in an equitable manner; and (3) to inculcate into students the nation's political and social democratic ideals. One of the main components of charter schools, as I understand them, is that these schools define their own purpose. I am very uneasy with this notion. I think private schools can choose their purpose but public schools, including public charter schools, need to be dedicated to an overall general purpose of schooling in a democracy.

I hope that all those involved in charter schools accept the responsibility of addressing the discrepancies between advantaged families and economically poor families in making school choices. I also hope the charter school movement steps up to the issue of the public purpose of schooling in a democracy. I consider these issues—segregation by class and the preparation of citizens—to be of the utmost concern, not only for our schools, but also for our society in general.

Reading this text and reflecting on how I was to develop this foreword has caused me to abandon my opposition to the public charter school movement and move into the supporter camp. I have come to believe that public charter schools can play a significant role in helping public education realize its role of providing all citizens the opportunity for a strong education that will enhance individual life chances while deepening democratic citizenship. Public charters can work on developing building-based learning communities that can usefully inform the work of other schools. The ability of charters to challenge rules and regulations may provide an opening for the educational community to reconsider special education law. The issues I raised about the public purpose of schooling and parent choice are pertinent to all public schools, charter or not.

—*Eugene Edgar*
Professor, College of Education, University of Washington

---

3. Parker, 2005, 344–51.

Acknowledgments

This volume is the result of many interviews, surveys, focus groups, and informal conversations. The authors wish to thank the parents, teachers, principals, scholars, and policy leaders across the country who generously contributed their time, insights, and observations to our research. We are indebted to special education experts Eileen Ahearn of the National Association of State Directors of Special Education, Joseph Gagnon of the University of Florida, Margaret McLaughlin of the University of Maryland, Christine Roch at Georgia State University, and Eugene Edgar at the Unversity of Washington, as well as Todd Ziebarth at the National Alliance for Public Charter Schools, who served as external reviewers for our working papers.

We are also grateful to program officers at the Bill & Melinda Gates Foundation who, three years ago, suspected that special education and charter schools was an important emerging policy issue and provided funding for the National Charter School Research Project to look into it. Our thanks as well to the Annie E. Casey Foundation for its support of this work. Great thanks, as always, goes to James Harvey, who helped pull our working papers series into a consistent and accessible form. Our editing and production team at the Center on Reinventing Public Education, led by Debra Britt, once again proved invaluable.

This research was funded by the Bill & Melinda Gates Foundation and the Annie E. Casey Foundation. We thank them for their support but acknowledge that the findings and conclusions presented here are those of the authors alone, and do not necessarily reflect the opinions of the foundations.

Introduction

ROBIN J. LAKE

This volume addresses choices made at the intersection of two very important policy arenas in education: special education and charter schools. As Tracey O'Brien and her colleagues argue in chapter 2, special education involves unique students and charters are unique kinds of public schools.

Advocates of school choice contend that the diversity of the student population requires a diversity of schools to allow parents to select the right fit for their children. Students with disabilities are diverse by their very nature, and their special and differing needs add layers of complexity to that diversity.[4] By definition, their needs are above and beyond those of their more typical peers.

Although the school choice and special education advocacy movements involve vastly different actors and histories, they share a common assumption. In both the theoretical frameworks shaping school choice and special education legal frameworks, it is intended that parents are full partners and advocates for their children in making educational choices. The responsibility of the family for making positive choices is thus magnified when families of students with special needs consider their range of options under a public school choice plan.

By law, charter schools are public schools with the same responsibilities to serve students with special needs as other public schools. On the other hand, charter schools are intentionally different from other public schools. They are freed from certain rules and regulations in order to deliver different and more effective educational programs to students. They are held accountable mainly by their results, not just for compliance in following regulatory requirements or seat time requirements. Those familiar with special education advocacy and law know that compliance with rules and process are often the focal point of legal challenge and enforcement. This can pose challenges to charter school founders who want to pursue unconventional approaches to serving students, but still stay true to the well-trodden legal foundations of federal special education

---

4. Within this volume, various terms are used for students with disabilities. Since there are differing opinions about terminology within the special education community, the editor deferred to the authors' preferences for their respective chapter(s). This report focuses on the children fitting the traditional definition for special education—those who face additional challenges in responding to the academic and social demands of school due to physical, cognitive, or emotional disabilities.

law. As one charter school advocate put it, when it comes to special education, charter schools are square pegs dealing with a round hole.

So the question naturally arises: how well are these unique kinds of schools serving these unique students? How many students with disabilities are attending charter schools? What kinds of special needs are served by charter schools? How do parents choose? How satisfied are they with their choices? And what do we know about the challenges and opportunities that special education legal frameworks create for charter school leaders?

To answer these questions, the National Charter School Research Project at the University of Washington's Center on Reinventing Public Education commissioned three in-depth papers to explore how special education issues present and work themselves out in a charter school environment.[5] The first paper, written by Tracey O'Brien, Kelly Hupfeld, and Paul Teske of the School of Public Affairs at the University of Colorado Denver, focused on how families with children with special needs perceive their options for charter schools and use them. The second paper, developed by Lauren Morando Rhim of Public Impact, was a detailed analysis of the obligations public schools are required to meet in addressing the needs of children with disabilities, and the challenges and opportunities those obligations present to charter schools. The third paper explored six charter schools across the United States that are successfully providing special services to students with a range of disabilities, from relatively mild to relatively severe. This paper was written by Rhim and Dana Brinson and complimented by a series of case studies by journalist and writer, Joanne Jacobs.

Each of these papers was detailed, impressive, and could readily have been extended into book-length form. Each merits a full reading from specialists on charter schools and special education. For the more general education reader, however, we thought the main points of these papers would be more accessible if the papers were broken up into chapter-length segments. This volume does just that, reshaping the first-rate material provided by these authors into eight chapters:

- Chapter 1 explores the complexities of special education requirements and reviews what is known about charter school success in working with students with special needs.
- Chapter 2 reviews what we know about charter schools and how parents make choices for their children.
- Chapter 3 presents new survey data about how parents of students with special needs make school choices for their children.

---

5. O'Brien, Hupfeld, and Teske, 2008; Rhim, 2008; and Rhim and Brinson, 2008. The complete papers are available on the Center on Reinventing Public Education website, www.crpe.org.

- Chapter 4 explores six case studies of charter school innovation and success around special education, providing insight into how students with disabilities can be served in new ways.
- Chapter 5 analyzes the common elements and promising practices among the six case study schools and asks whether traditional public schools could adopt these practices or whether they are a function of the autonomy afforded by charter laws.
- Detailed analysis of the challenges and opportunities in special education for charter schools is presented in chapters 6 and 7.
- Chapter 8 pulls the discussion together and explores the implications of these findings, both for charter schools and the students with special needs that they serve.

What seems clear is that the diversity of offerings in the charter school landscape can be important for many children with special needs. Even students facing quite severe challenges can be well served by well-designed charter school programs. Most parents, based on the evidence here, report being satisfied with the special education services received by their children in charter schools. In fact, some charter schools have an informal reputation as havens for children with special needs.

However, charter schools are not viewed as silver bullets by parents of children with special needs. Instead, they represent one option in a landscape of choices that must be examined carefully. In addition, parents of children with special needs can be said to experience a choice process that is ongoing. The selection of a single school is but a point in the journey. Parents of these children see themselves as needing to be ever watchful, monitoring whether their child is being served well in the school they have chosen and engaging in ongoing negotiations with school staff. If the school is not working out, the parents stand ready to change schools again.

Due to the special vulnerability of their children and the due process rights built into special education statutes, parents of children with special needs are hyper-choosers. They seek, and have the power of law behind them in searching for it, the precise fit for their children's unique, and often highly complex, needs. The diversity and innovation charter schools provide in the ways they approach special education represent an important addition to the public education landscape for these parents. Some charters have used their autonomy to create especially effective approaches, some of which are potential new models for public education writ large.

Chapter 1

Special Education Requirements and Charter Schools

L AUREN M ORANDO R HIM

S pecial education and related services represent a collection of programs and supports developed to help children with disabilities access and succeed in school. Public schools, including charter schools, are required to adhere to all federal civil rights laws, including the Individuals with Disabilities Education Act (IDEA) of 2004, Section 504 of the Rehabilitation Act of 1973, and the Americans with Disabilities Act (ADA) of 1990, which were developed to protect the civil rights of individuals with disabilities. While Section 504 and ADA establish a basic foundation for *access* to public education, the IDEA establishes specific guidelines regarding *educating* children with disabilities and provides financial support to states to help them implement the law. Consequently, while Section 504 and ADA apply to public schools (as they do to all public facilities), most discussion regarding educating children with disabilities focuses on IDEA rules and regulations.

Congress passed the Education for All Handicapped Children Act, P.L. 94-142, the precursor to IDEA, in 1975. The law represented a major shift in the conceptualization of the notion of disability and the integration of children with disabilities into public education and the larger society. IDEA and related regulations emphasize that public schools, including charter schools, are responsible for educating students with disabilities and providing a "free appropriate public education" in the "least restrictive environment." A written plan to provide special education services, the individualized education program (IEP), is developed by a small team comprised of administrators, teachers, specialists, and the student's parents. An IEP is the tool used to outline a school's plan to realize those core tenets of special education—a free and appropriate public education offered in the least restrictive environment—for each child eligible for special education.[6]

---

6. These principles were developed in response to a history, prior to 1975, in which states and local districts frequently refused to provide special services or make accommodations for students with disabilities, particularly those with the most severe cognitive and physical challenges. Other states and districts insisted that special education services, when offered, be provided in separate classrooms.

The definitions of these principles are multi-dimensional and have been the focus of extensive litigation, including multiple influential Supreme Court cases.[7] In its simplest form, the guarantee of a free and appropriate public education aims to ensure that children with disabilities will receive, without cost, the services and programs selected by the individualized education program team to meet students' individual needs. The notion of "appropriate" has been the subject of particularly contentious litigation aimed at defining the extent of services required to meet this standard. It has generally been interpreted to include a very broad continuum of services and supports required to allow a child with a disability access to the general education curriculum.

The construct, "least restrictive environment," reflects a fundamental conviction that all children should be educated in the general education classroom alongside their peers without disabilities, with appropriate aids and supports, unless they cannot succeed in this environment. Based on the core civil rights principle that "separate" by definition cannot be equal, the least restrictive environment reflects a commitment to educating children with disabilities alongside their peers without disabilities. In contrast to historic practice wherein children with disabilities were initially placed in separate schools or classrooms and thereafter had to demonstrate the ability to succeed in the general education classroom in order to be integrated or "mainstreamed," this principle holds that all children are initially presumed to be able to be educated in the general education classroom. They are only pulled out of the general education classroom as dictated by their individual needs as articulated in the individualized education program. Furthermore, separate services and placements should include opportunities to interact with peers without disabilities to the maximum extent possible. Depending on a child's particular disability, and in accordance with their individualized education program, meeting the standard of the two principles together (least restrictive environment and free and appropriate public education) ranges on a continuum from being educated 100 percent of the school day in a general education classroom with minimal special aids and supports to 100 percent of the day in a private residential setting with extensive services.

Educating children with a wide array of disabilities and complying with sometimes onerous federal and state special education procedural requirements with finite resources can be a challenge for all public schools, traditional and charter.[8] The 2002 President's Commission on Excellence in Special Education documented multiple challenges associated with IDEA. In line with how society

---

7. For an extensive listing and analysis of special education case law, see Wrightslaw: http://www.wrightslaw.com/caselaw.htm.

8. President's Commission on Excellence in Special Education, 2002.

has typically conceptualized individuals with disabilities, special education supports and services are generally conceived of as something distinctly separate as opposed to an integral part of the instructional program. Furthermore, efforts to monitor and control expenditure of special education dollars and adherence to due process have created a system that focuses more on process than performance. For instance, in large part due to limitations associated with funding streams, special education services have typically only been provided once academic failure has been documented, as opposed to as a preventive strategy—loosely equivalent to waiting for someone to hit the ground before extending them a helping hand that could potentially prevent the fall.

Compounding the challenges associated with an overly bureaucratic process is the practical reality that there is a relatively limited research base on effective instructional strategies for children with a diverse range of abilities and a shortage of qualified special education teachers available to educate these children. In response to these documented challenges, the 2002 Commission outlined three broad recommendations to improve IDEA and, consequently, the education of children with disabilities: (1) focus on results, not on process; (2) embrace a model of prevention rather than failure; and (3) consider children with disabilities as general education children first. These broad themes influenced the reauthorization of IDEA in 2004.

As a society we have witnessed improvements in the lives of individuals with disabilities during the last 30 years, but public schools and society at large have not progressed to the point that individuals with disabilities can enjoy a "fully normalized, fair life experience."[9] P.L. 94-142 required that students with disabilities have access to neighborhood schools and general education classrooms with appropriate supports and services. With the reauthorization of IDEA, coupled with the accountability requirements of *No Child Left Behind* (NCLB), requirements associated with access and due process are no longer the ceiling, but rather the floor, of expectations for students with disabilities. Public schools are now held accountable for demonstrating that the sub-group of children with disabilities is making adequate yearly progress (AYP) analogous to their peers without disabilities.

Although much controversy and consternation whirls around NCLB requirements related to AYP, and specifically the challenges of assessing children with a diverse range of disabilities, the law undoubtedly has forced states, districts, and schools to focus more attention on ensuring that their students with disabilities are provided access to the general education curriculum and prepared to take state assessments.[10]

---

9. Andrews et al., 2000.

10. National Council on Disability, 2008.

While acknowledging the gains achieved since 1975, the current system of educating students with disabilities in public schools arguably does not meet the goals underlying the federal statutes. In particular, schools struggle to hire and retain qualified special education personnel and more resources are required to provide adequate supports and develop new instructional approaches.[11] The result of these inadequacies is that many students enrolled in special education programs have less than ideal school experiences, drop out, or do not obtain the skills required to graduate and succeed.[12]

Most advocates agree that in order to address these persistent shortfalls, schools will need to carry out special education in new and different ways. What kind of "new and different" approaches hold most promise is a subject of great debate even within the disability advocacy community. In that context, there is a strong case for experimentation with different strategies for change, coupled with rigorous evaluation and accountability for results with students. Initiating change may be particularly difficult in large school systems with established standard operating procedures. Charter schools present an important opportunity to accelerate change, experiment, and advance the knowledge base related to educating children with disabilities. However, to realize the potential opportunity, charter schools must first overcome specific challenges associated with their unique charter status.

LEGAL IDENTITY OF CHARTER SCHOOLS

When the charter sector first started to evolve in the early 1990s there was both concern and hope expressed by analysts regarding the degree to which (1) charter schools would welcome children with disabilities, (2) special education would be too heavy a financial and procedural burden for fledging charter schools, and (3) the charter sector could create new opportunities for all children, including children with disabilities.[13]

The charter sector has since evolved out of infancy and into young adulthood but concerns about educating children with disabilities in the sector persist. Yet, we now have experience and a growing body of research to draw from to better to understand how educating children with disabilities presents challenges to the charter sector. Furthermore, the experiences and research reveal multiple opportunities to address the challenges to ensure that children with disabilities can access the over 4,000 charter schools currently operating and succeed in them.

---

11. Ibid.

12. Andrews et al., 2000; National Council on Disability, 2008.

13. Ahearn et al., 2001; Fiore and Cashman, 1998; Fiore, Warren, and Cashman, 1998; Heubert, 1997; Lange, 1997; McKinney and Mead, 1996; McLaughlin and Henderson, 1998; Mead, 1995; Medler and Nathan, 1995; Szabo and Gerber, 1996.

A key defining legal characteristic of a charter school is whether it is a local education agency (LEA) or part of a larger LEA.[14] Twelve states' charter laws dictate that charter schools are independent LEAs and eighteen states' charter laws dictate that charters are schools within an existing LEA. Charter laws in the remaining ten states and Washington, D.C., dictate that legal status is determined based on who authorizes the school or the type of charter school created, or they grant schools the option to elect to be either part of an LEA or their own LEA.[15] Nationwide, approximately 60 percent of all charter schools are LEAs and the remaining 40 percent are part of an LEA.[16]

Legal identity is a critical variable in relation to special education because responsibility for fulfilling legal requirements is mostly assigned to LEAs by states, not to the individual schools of an LEA. If a charter school is part of an LEA, the major responsibility for special education remains with the district, although some sharing of that responsibility between the school and its district can be negotiated. If the charter school is its own LEA, however, it is responsible for all IDEA requirements that apply to all districts. For example, districts and LEAs are responsible for identifying children with disabilities, following all procedures and timelines associated with evaluations, developing individualized education programs, and providing the full continuum of educational settings as defined in the least restrictive environment regulations. A charter school that is its own LEA assumes all these obligations.

Further complicating the issue is the fact that under some charter statutes, a charter school's LEA status for special education may be different from its LEA status for other purposes, such as receipt of federal Title I funds.[17] So, special education responsibilities are vast and the onus of fulfilling the responsibilities is particularly heavy for charter schools that are independent LEAs.

With that information as background, what does the profile of special education in the charter sector look like?

ENROLLMENT OF CHILDREN WITH DISABILITIES

Children with disabilities represent approximately 11.51 percent of the total enrollment in public schools nationwide.[18] Data from the charter sector indicate that 10.6 percent of charter school students had an individualized education program during the 2003–04 school year.[19] Data from a national survey

---

14. Green and Mead, 2004; Heubert, 1997; Rhim, Ahearn, and Lange, 2007.

15. Ahearn et al., 2005.

16. Rhim et al., 2007a.

17. Green and Mead, 2004.

18. U.S. Department of Education, Office of Special Education Programs, Data Analysis System, 2006.

19. Rhim et al., 2007a.

as well as state-specific research documented that enrollment of children with disabilities in charter schools ranges from 0 percent in some schools to 100 percent in a small sub-group of charter schools developed primarily for students with disabilities.[20] This variation is true of traditional public schools as well. Although school districts have a legal obligation to serve all students, special education enrollment within a school district can vary tremendously.

Counseling out children with disabilities—whether due to lack of awareness of responsibilities or an intentional desire to limit the number of children in special education—remains a concern in the charter sector.[21] Conversely, there is evidence that some charter schools are reporting smaller proportions of children with disabilities because they are providing effective early interventions or offering an educational program that reduces the need to label children.[22]

Children with disabilities are identified as having 1 of 13 categories of disabilities (i.e., specific learning disabilities, speech or language impairments, mental retardation, emotional disturbance, other health impairments, multiple disabilities, hearing impairments, orthopedic impairments, visual impairments, autism, deaf-blindness, traumatic brain injury, and developmental delay). Students are also more loosely categorized as having a "high-incidence" disability (e.g., a common type of disability such as a specific learning or speech/language disability) or a "low-incidence" disability (e.g., an uncommon disability such as traumatic brain injury, autism, or orthopedic impairment). The high-incidence group includes approximately 90 percent of all children with disabilities.[23]

Although national data are not available for charter schools, an analysis of enrollments in California charter schools documented that, according to type of disability, the proportions of students enrolling differ from state averages. Most notably, charter schools enrolled more students with specific learning disabilities (61 percent compared to 55 percent) and fewer students with mental retardation (2 percent compared to 6 percent) than traditional public schools.[24]

SPECIAL EDUCATION SERVICE PROVISION

Multiple qualitative analyses have documented that charter schools tend to serve more of their students with disabilities in general education classrooms.[25] A survey of a random sample of charter schools nationwide documented that 73 percent of students with disabilities are in the general education classroom

---

20. Guarino and Chau, 2003; Miron and Nelson, 2002; Rhim et al., 2007a.

21. Ibid.

22. Finn, Manno, and Bierlein, 1996; Sullins and Miron, 2005.

23. President's Commission on Excellence in Special Education, 2002.

24. Rhim, Faukner, and McLaughlin, 2006.

25. Fiore, Warren, and Cashman, 1998; Guarino and Chau, 2003; Ahearn et al., 2001; Rhim et al., 2006.

at least 80 percent of the day.[26] This is in contrast to all public schools nation-wide that include 50 percent of students with disabilities in general education classrooms, 80 percent of the day or more.[27] While the survey data documented that more children with disabilities are being educated in relatively less restrictive environments than typical in traditional public schools, multiple qualitative studies have raised questions about the degree to which charter schools have the financial or instructional capacity to provide adequate supports in general education classrooms.[28] We know very little about the degree to which the students with disabilities who are spending most of their day in general education classrooms are receiving the aids, supports, and services required for them to succeed.

ACADEMIC ACCOUNTABILITY AND OUTCOMES

Charter schools are subject to the same accountability requirements as traditional public schools. They must administer annual assessments and track adequate yearly progress (AYP). In addition, they are subject to periodic compliance monitoring by their respective state department of education under IDEA. Aside from systemic accountability mechanisms dictated by NCLB and IDEA, charter schools are held accountable under state charter statutes that provide charter schools authority to operate under renewable charters or contracts. They are also held accountable by parents who choose the school. Parents of children with disabilities can file due process complaints if the school does not uphold the policies and procedures outlined in IDEA or related state special education statutes.

To date, very little research has been conducted on the academic outcomes of students with disabilities in charter schools. The lack of research is due in large part to the small average size of most charter schools (i.e., 309 students)[29] relative to traditional public schools (i.e., 552 students),[30] and the small number of students with disabilities in most charter schools. Under NCLB guidelines adopted in individual states, reporting on the sub-groups is frequently omitted because of the minimum group size required to ensure statistical reliability and to protect students' privacy. Evidence from the previously mentioned analyses of California charter schools indicated that students with disabilities are performing as well as, if not slightly better than, their peers in traditional public schools. Specifically, while traditional public schools in California overall

---

26. Rhim et al., 2007a.

27. U.S. Department of Education, 2005.

28. Ahearn et al., 2001; Arsen, Plank, and Sykes, 1999; Fiore, Warren, and Cashman, 1998; McKinney, 1996.

29. Rhim et al., 2007a.

30. U.S. Department of Education, National Center for Education Statistics, 2007.

outperformed charter schools (e.g., 60 percent of traditional public schools meet AYP vs. 55 percent of charter schools) and scored higher on the California Academic Performance Index (696 vs. 648), children with disabilities in charter schools were performing at a higher level than children with disabilities in traditional public schools.

That is to say, more students with disabilities in California charter schools achieved "Proficient" and "Advanced" compared to their peers in traditional public schools in English language arts (13.73 percent compared to 9.96 percent) and mathematics (14.40 percent compared to 13.23 percent). The differences were present even when analyzed according to disability category across the two types of schools.[31] The study of California charter schools had notable limitations (e.g., point in time vs. longitudinal analysis, limited student-level data, and a substantial difference between enrollments in traditional vs. charter schools). Nevertheless, it does provide interesting findings regarding academic achievement for students with disabilities in California charter schools that may have implications for the broader sector.

CONCLUSION

The research to date on educating students with disabilities in the charter sector is neither broad nor deep. However, it does provide a basic descriptive foundation for future research.

In sum:

- Charter schools are required by statute to adhere to all the civil rights guarantees laid out in IDEA, including providing a free and appropriate public education in the least restrictive environment through an individualized education program.
- Meeting onerous federal and state statutes and regulations around special education can be a challenge for all schools, traditional and charter.
- Charter schools face an even more complicated legal environment, based on whether they are part of a local education agency (which assumes responsibility for meeting state regulations governing special education) or are their own LEA (in which case the charter school assumes the LEA's responsibility).
- It appears that charter schools enroll a smaller proportion of students with disabilities than do regular public schools (10.6 percent vs. 11.51 percent) and, in California, enroll a higher proportion of students with less severe

---

31. Rhim, Faukner, and McLaughlin, 2006.

"high-incidence disabilities" such as learning disabilities than do traditional public schools (e.g., 61 percent vs. 55 percent) and a smaller proportion of "low-incidence disabilities" such as retardation or autism than do traditional public schools (2 percent vs. 6 percent).

• To date, very little national research has been conducted on the academic outcomes of students with disabilities in charter schools, but evidence from one state study indicated that students with disabilities in charter schools are performing at least as well as, if not better than, their peers in traditional public schools.

Against this backdrop, what does the latest research have to tell us about how parents choose schools for their children with special needs and how satisfied they are with the choices they make?

Chapter 2

Parent Choice and Charter Schools

TRACEY O'BRIEN, KELLY HUPFELD, AND PAUL TESKE

Charter schools are public schools authorized by state law to operate under a contract, or charter, with a charter authorizer (a school district, institution of higher education, or a state, for example). Currently, 40 states and the District of Columbia permit the formation of charter schools.

A charter school is generally given autonomy and freedom from specified state and local rules that otherwise apply to public schools, and its authorizer decides whether or not the school's subsequent performance warrants extension or termination of the contract. This autonomy allows charter schools to provide a wide variety of instructional and curricular approaches that may not be available in traditional public schools. As a result, there is no "typical" charter school. The focus of a charter school may be anything from a Montessori approach to a school serving primarily pregnant teenagers. As public schools, charter schools are held accountable not only to their authorizer but also under state and federal accountability laws.

Charter schools have proven popular and their ranks have grown. The National Charter School Research Project estimates that there are over 4,000 charter schools operating in the United States, serving more than 1.2 million students.[32] This compares to about 90,000 traditional public schools, serving more than 50 million students. California has the greatest number of charter schools, with an estimated 710 schools. Some states, such as Washington, by contrast, have no charter schools.

In general, parents are more satisfied with schools when they are able to choose the schools themselves.[33] Charter schools are schools of choice—they are not assigned students by the local school district. Instead, they must attract families by convincing them that the school represents a good educational choice for their children. In other words, serving students well would seem to be the means by which charter schools survive.

---

32. Lake, 2008.
33. Buckley and Schneider, 2006.

Past state-level surveys of parent satisfaction with charter schools reveal most parents to be very satisfied.[34] A study of charter school parents in the District of Columbia found that charter school parents ranked their schools more highly than did parents of children enrolled in traditional public schools;[35] however, the same study found that parent satisfaction with charter schools declined over time, so that satisfaction levels with both charter and traditional public schools ended up at similar levels.

Paul Teske and Robert Reichardt looked at choices made by charter school parents in Milwaukee and Denver, as well as in the District of Columbia.[36] They found that the decisionmaking process of parents who ultimately chose charter schools was very similar to the decisionmaking process of parents making other choices. Like other parents, charter school parents relied on information sources such as other parents, school visits, and reviewing printed and web-based materials. That said, parents who ultimately chose charter schools were more likely to be satisfied with their choice than were parents who chose traditional public schools.

SPECIAL EDUCATION IN ALL PUBLIC SCHOOLS

Special education serves a category of students deemed to have needs above and beyond the typical student. A dense framework of federal and state laws and regulations governs the provision of special education services to ensure students receive the services they need. Although gifted and talented students are often covered in the same statutes, this book focuses on the children fitting the traditional definition for special education—those who face additional challenges in responding to the academic and social demands of school due to physical, cognitive, or emotional disabilities.

Nationwide, approximately 11.51 percent of students in all public schools receive special education services.[37] The range of disabilities eligible for special education services is wide. For example, some children in public schools have severe physical disabilities that confine them to a wheelchair; others are blind or deaf; others are mentally retarded or severely autistic. Other children have more "hidden" disabilities, such as learning disabilities, processing disorders, or relatively minor speech impediments. These students may need only a few accommodations or special services provided for a time to participate in the typical educational program. Frequently, children will present multiple disabilities. This wide range of disabilities means that it is virtually impossible to find a single way

---

34. See, e.g., McCully and Malin, 2003.
35. Buckley and Schneider, 2006.
36. Teske and Reichardt, 2006.
37. U.S. Department of Education, Office of Special Education Programs, Data Analysis System, 2006.

to effectively educate all children with special needs; instead, their educational program must be individualized to meet the needs of their specific disorders. In fact, federal law requires an individualized program for students with disabilities.

The federal Individuals with Disabilities Education Act (IDEA) contains extensive procedural requirements that mandate the involvement of parents in making decisions about the education of children with special needs. Parents must be involved, for example, in the drafting of an individualized education program (IEP) that identifies the services the child will receive along with individualized goals and indicators of progress. Parents are entitled to bring legal action to enforce their rights and the rights of their children under IDEA to a free education in the least restrictive environment appropriate to their child's needs.

While this process was designed to end the practice of schools effectively ignoring the needs of children with disabilities, it has been criticized as setting up an often adversarial relationship between parents and their child's school. Parents and schools may differ on what services are appropriate to meet the needs of the child, with schools and districts often cognizant of budget issues and parents focusing solely on the needs of their child. Parents familiar with the IEP process and their rights under IDEA also likely pay particular attention to the school's "fit" with their child's unique needs.

A national survey conducted in 2002 by Public Agenda found that two-thirds of parents with special-needs children in public schools were satisfied with their children's schools, rating the school as doing an excellent or good job of giving their child the help he or she needed.[38] Thirteen percent described their school as doing a poor job of providing services. One in six parents surveyed had considered a lawsuit against the district, and as many as one-third of the parents of children with severe needs had considered lawsuits. These results are consistent with prior findings.[39]

Special education parents are dissatisfied with their schools for many reasons, including disagreements with school staff about the needs of their child, concern over the quality and breadth of delivery of special education services, feelings of powerlessness or disrespect, lack of communication, or lack of trust.[40] Parents want to know that the school views their child as an individual with his or her own strengths and weaknesses.

The Public Agenda survey also found that nearly seven in ten parents agreed that there is much less stigma attached to special education today. In the past,

---

38. In comparison, 59 percent of parents of students in grades K–12, without regard to special education status, report being "very satisfied" with their child's school. Of parents with children in public schools, 55 percent of parents whose children attended an assigned school reported being very satisfied, and 63 percent of parents in chosen public schools were very satisfied. Herrold and O'Donnell, 2008.

39. Newman, 2005.

40. Lake and Billingsley, 2000.

parents often fought the identification of their child as eligible for special education, fearing that the label alone would have a deleterious effect on their child's future. Today, many children are eligible for special education as a result of learning disabilities or other hidden disorders such as attention deficit disorders. In fact, specific learning disabilities and speech and language disorders make up the majority of special education diagnoses today.[41] Parents understand that an IEP gains these children extra academic attention and accommodations on important tests, benefits that may outweigh any stigma.

SPECIAL EDUCATION IN CHARTER SCHOOLS

It should be clear from the prior discussion that both charter schools and children with special education needs are unique. These children have needs that are outside the traditional parameters of public education, and these schools are operating outside the parameters applicable to traditional public schools. How do these populations intersect?

As mentioned above, students eligible for special education services make up approximately 11.51 percent of the public school population. Similarly, in 2003–04, approximately 11 percent of charter school students received special education services.[42] Of these, 10.3 percent were identified as having severe disabilities.[43] Charter schools were created in part to find new ways to serve at-risk students and, in 2003–04, 8 percent of charter schools reported serving primarily students with behavioral problems compared to 4 percent of traditional public schools.[44] Three percent of charter school operators reported being set up to serve student with disabilities;[45] however, "[t]here is virtually no difference in the rates at which charter school principals and traditional public school principals report an emphasis on special education . . . ."[46]

Previous literature has focused on the real and perceived difficulties of charter schools in delivering special education services.[47] Charter schools, like all public schools, may not refuse otherwise eligible students on the basis of their need for special education services, yet sometimes the delivery of special education services can be more difficult for charter schools. Special education services are traditionally delivered as part of the bundle of services a district provides

---

41. U.S. Department of Education, National Center for Education Statistics, 2008.
42. Ziebarth, 2007.
43. Rhim, Lange, Ahearn, and McLaughlin, 2007a.
44. Ibid.
45. Ibid.
46. Christensen and Lake, 2007.
47. See, e.g., Rhim, Lange, Ahearn, and McLaughlin, 2006.

to its schools. However, in the case of charter schools, this relationship is not automatically assumed.

Lauren Morando Rhim et al. found that practice and policy regarding charter schools and special education varied widely among states.[48] In some states, charter schools are solely responsible for delivery of special education services. In others, delivery of services to students in charter schools is the responsibility of the school district, or is a shared responsibility between the district and the school. Depending on their situations, charter schools may enter into a contract for services with the local district, or may form regional cooperatives for this purpose. The flow of state dollars for special education also varies widely, with funding in some states going directly to the charter schools and in some states going directly to districts.

State-level officials in charge of charter schools report that charters experience many difficulties in providing special education services, including inadequate funding, complex legal and procedural requirements, challenges working with parents, and struggles to find qualified special education teachers.

Yet there is obviously something about charter schools that is leading many parents of students with special needs to choose these schools, especially those families whose children have milder disabilities. Prior studies that took place in the early years of the charter school movement shed some light on the reasons behind these choices.

In a national study of charter schools and special education, researchers visited 32 charter schools in 15 states and conducted focus groups of administrators, teachers, parents, and students.[49] The study found that parents of students with significant special needs tended not to enroll them in charter schools, except for those few schools specifically designed to educate these students. Instead, students with special needs in charter schools typically tend to have milder disabilities, such as learning disabilities.

Parents in this study most often cited the negative aspects of their prior (non-charter) school as reasons for switching to charter schools. At over half of the schools visited, parents cited a general dissatisfaction with the prior school. Dissatisfaction with the special education program at the prior school was an equally popular reason for changing schools.

The positive characteristics of charter schools were also important to parents, although not to the same degree as the negative characteristics of the prior school. At one-third of the schools, parents cited the charter school's small size or small class size. Factors such as the school's curricular focus or instructional approach, the quality of the staff, the school's reputation, a safe

---

48. Rhim, Lange, Ahearn, and McLaughlin, 2007a.
49. Fiore, 2000.

and community-like environment, and individualized attention were each mentioned at one-fourth of the schools.

Also in 2000, Cheryl M. Lange and Camilla A. Lehr observed significantly more special-needs students in Minnesota charter schools than have been documented in other studies.[50] Twenty-six percent of parents in the charter schools studied reported having one or more children receiving special education services at the charter school, and thirty-six percent of these children had been identified as having learning disabilities.

Parents of children with disabilities ranked the following factors as *significantly more important* to their school choice decision than did parents of children without disabilities:

- special education services available at the charter school;
- the special needs of their child;
- dissatisfaction with a prior school; and
- the need for their child to have a fresh start.

Reasons listed as *important or very important* to their decision to attend the charter school by parents of students with special needs included class size, staff members, academic programming, special education services, school philosophy, discipline policy, school safety, the special needs of the child, and the number of students at the school.

A more limited study involved interviews with a total of six parents and five administrators from two charter schools in Texas.[51] It revealed similar themes. Parents reported that the needs of their children had not been met in traditional school settings, which had resulted in emotional distress and academic difficulties for the children. When the children moved to charter school settings, their emotional and academic situations improved. Although the parents reported ongoing difficulties with underprepared teachers, they felt they had more influence over this situation in the charter schools than they had in the public schools.

In brief, the literature reveals a situation in which parents of students with special needs have the force of law behind them in demanding special services for their children. Many of them find what they seek in traditional public schools, but a substantial number of parents increasingly seek out a charter school alternative. The alternatives are not always perfect, but many parents report that despite ongoing difficulties they feel the smaller charter school environment is more appropriate for their children and that they have a greater say in their children's educational program.

The next chapter provides greater insight into how parents of children with special needs view charter schools.

---

50. Lange and Lehr, 2000.
51. Shields, 2005.

Chapter 3

How Parents of Students with Special Needs Choose Schools

Tracey O'Brien, Kelly Hupfeld, and Paul Teske

To explore how parents choose schools, this study examined parental choice in two medium-sized urban districts, Denver and Milwaukee, each of which is well known nationally for its relatively extensive experience with school choice and diverse student populations. Colorado and Wisconsin have 144 and 226 charter schools respectively, and rank high in the perceived "strength" of their charter school laws.[52] In each of the cities, three focus groups were held with parents of students with special needs. Parent focus group participants were recruited in Denver through a variety of networks and support groups that exist for parents of children with special needs. The leaders of these groups assisted researchers by providing flyers and other sign-up opportunities for group members. Focus groups in Milwaukee were recruited through charter schools and through contracting with local consultants for identification and recruitment of parents meeting the study criteria.

In Denver, participation ranged from 10 to 12 participants at each group. One group consisted primarily of parents of children with special needs attending traditional schools; another group consisted entirely of parents of children with special needs attending charter schools; and the final group had a mix of parents from each school setting. Parents in Denver's all-charter school group were Spanish-speaking, and that group was conducted in Spanish and their discussion translated. In Milwaukee, poor weather contributed to lower turnout. Nine parents participated in a mixed group of charter and traditional school parents; five parents attended a charter school-only group; and five parents attended a traditional school-only group.

Surveys were also distributed to parents of children with special needs in Denver and Milwaukee, primarily through the charter schools their students attended, but also through networks for parents of children with special needs. The survey was intended for parents of children in charter schools, but researchers also received responses from parents of children in traditional schools, albeit

---

52. Consoletti, 2008.

Denver and Milwaukee Public Schools

Both Denver and Milwaukee have a long history of school choice, with state charter schools laws passed in Colorado and Wisconsin in 1993.

In the 2007–08 school year, the Denver Public Schools (DPS) enrolled more than 73,000 students at 151 schools, including 21 charter schools and 7 alternative schools. Many families in DPS exercise school choice. According to the Colorado Department of Education, over 6,000 students residing in DPS choiced out to other districts and the statewide Charter School Institute, while about 4,800 students choiced in from other districts. The charter schools in DPS serve just under 10 percent of the student population.

Milwaukee Public Schools (MPS) has a notable variety of schools under its jurisdiction that serve its 87,000 students. Most schools (136) are "traditional," although the variety of traditional schools ranges from language immersion to Montessori-based to expeditionary learning and arts focuses. There are six alternative programs at the secondary level. Thirty-one schools are partnership schools, private schools at the secondary level that are run by nonprofit organizations to serve at-risk students. Four schools are contract schools. Milwaukee's 37 charter schools serve 15 percent of its students. Nearly 19,000 students attend 122 private schools in Milwaukee using vouchers issued through the district's Milwaukee Parent Choice Program, and around 6,600 students who live in the city attend public schools in the suburbs through Wisconsin's open enrollment system.

at a much lower ratio. The survey was not intended to represent a random sample of parents, but rather to serve as an extension of information gathered from focus groups. Responses were received from a total of 227 parents, 116 in Denver and 111 in Milwaukee. Of the respondents, 191 were parents of students with special needs at charter schools and 34 were parents of students with special needs at traditional schools.

OVERVIEW OF STUDY FINDINGS

The focus groups painted a picture of parents faced with a dizzying array of choices. Within that range of choices, they undertake a treasure hunt to find the elusive school that will serve their child willingly and well. Once they find a school, their work is not over as they monitor services and advocate for their child at school and with the district. If a school is not working out as hoped, the difficult search begins again.

This apparently endless process has different effects on different people. Many of the parents have accepted their roles as dogged and determined advocates for their children. A few others seem to have given up, defeated by repeated frustration. Put simply, the school choice process can be more complex for parents of children with special needs. It is difficult to generalize about what

> "Parents of special-needs children have to look at schools differently. We can't just send our children to any school."—*Milwaukee parent*

these parents are looking for in a school, because what they are looking for is whatever their child needs in a school, which varies widely from child to child.

The same may be said of typical children, but it is more so for these special-needs children. These children are fragile, whether physically, intellectually, or socially. Their parents feel very keenly the responsibility to make sure these children are safe and cared for.

If we are to generalize about what parents of special-needs children are looking for in a school, the following list probably works well:

- They want the school to *fit* their child, so that the child can be part of the school community with all the social and emotional benefits of community membership.
- They want the school to *want* their child, not to view their different child as a burden that interferes with educating typical children.
- They want the *right academic program* for their child, one that will strike a balance between ensuring any necessary accommodations and ensuring that their child achieves his or her potential.
- They want *consistent and thorough communications* with and among all staff who have responsibility for their child, including classroom aides, teachers, principals, and district staff.

HOW DO PARENTS OF STUDENTS WITH SPECIAL NEEDS CHOOSE?

One would expect, given the array of choices discussed during the focus groups, that parents responding to the survey would report that they considered several schools for their child, if not a large number of schools. The expectation would not be met; most survey respondents reported that they did not consider other schools when making the choice about their children's current school. Just 34 percent reported considering other schools.

This is a surprising finding and stands in contrast to Paul Teske and Robert Reichardt's earlier findings that over 70 percent of parents choosing schools had considered a number of schools.[53] One factor that may be at work in this study is the income level of parents. More than half of survey respondents reported family income below $40,000, with 20 percent reporting income above $80,000. Just 23 percent of parents with incomes under $40,000 and

---

53. Teske and Reichardt, 2006.

35 percent of parents with incomes between $40,000 and $80,000 reported looking at other schools. Conversely, 71 percent of parents with incomes above $80,000 looked at other schools. Higher-income parents also reported more often that their children had previously attended other schools.

So, one factor may be income. Higher income may provide options in the form of transportation and day-care arrangements not available to low-income parents. However, the choice process itself may be different for special education parents. That is to say that while the initial search may be just as complex, ultimately the range of potentially attractive schools is very limited. For example, in some cases, parents may not consider a number of schools because the choice of school is fairly obvious: it may be, for example, the only school with an autism program. Thus, parent respondents may have interpreted "considering other schools" as requiring an ultimate determination, after much research, that more than one school would be appropriate for their child.

Nearly one-third of parents (32 percent) ended up choosing the school closest to their home. This finding is consistent with the results obtained by Paul Teske et al. in looking at lower- to middle-income parent choice in Denver, Milwaukee, and Washington, D.C.[54]

What Sources of Information Are Used?

Like other parents choosing schools, parents of students with disabilities have a wide variety of information sources they use in selecting a school for their children. We asked parents to identify how they heard about their current school, and they indicated the following sources of information:

- Other parents: 37 percent
- Teachers/school staff: 19 percent
- School is our neighborhood school: 19 percent
- District referral: 16 percent
- Open house: 9 percent
- District website: 4 percent
- District mailing 4 percent
- Nonprofit group: 4 percent
- Community meeting: 2 percent
- Doctor/therapist: 1 percent

These results are reasonably consistent with results obtained by Teske et al.,[55] although they show somewhat more reliance on other parents and somewhat less reliance on district websites and printed information (perhaps reflecting

---

54. Teske et al., 2007.
55. Ibid.

the need of these parents for more individualized information). Other sources of information spontaneously offered by parents included family members, organizations that help identify children with disabilities (such as ChildFind or Denver Options in Denver), and personal visits. It appeared from survey results that Hispanic parents were most likely to get their information from their social networks.

When parents were asked to identify which information sources were *most helpful* in making their decisions, most parents identified other parents and teachers as their most important resources. Focus group discussions clarified this result. Many focus group participants reported that they did "research" (such as talking to other parents, visiting websites, etc.) to identify potential school candidates based on school reputation and word of mouth, and then engaged in an extensive school visiting process. Ultimately, many parents reported that the school visit made the biggest impression on them.

For example, focus group parents in Milwaukee reported that visiting schools allowed them to see class sizes and how teachers interacted with children. One Denver parent reported researching schools online, and then visiting eight or nine schools. Another parent reported selecting two schools to consider and then visiting each school eight times before making her decision. Parents of students who will be in self-contained classrooms reported visiting those class-rooms to see whether the other students in the classroom would be appropriate peers for their children. In general, parents needed to "feel" the atmosphere of the school in order to understand whether that school was right for their children. This may be true whether the parent felt they had ten viable school options or just one.

The value of district staff in parental decisionmaking varied substantially between the two cities. Parents in Milwaukee seemed to regard their district staff as knowledgeable and helpful, if not always the last word on the right school. For example, Milwaukee has an autism consultant who has been known to drive parents around to different prospective schools. On the other hand, Denver parents did not view district special education staff as a resource in selecting schools. These parents commented that "[a]dministrators are very guarded. They don't want to say or do anything wrong." Denver parents also perceived the district to be more concerned about the issues of low-income children as a group, while special education children receive lower priority.

Although the educational foundation of school programs was certainly important to many parents, only one focus group parent reported looking at school test scores, such as those found on Colorado's School Accountability Reports or the Wisconsin School Performance Report. This may be due to parental perceptions that their child, by definition, is not average, so it doesn't really matter how the average child at the school performs, or even how the average special education student performs.

Survey respondents were asked whether there was any information they needed or wanted but did not have at the time they made their school decisions. Overall, parents felt they had the information they needed. Just 11 percent of parents thought they were missing information when they made their decisions. However, this statistic appeared to vary by income and education levels (although not by ethnicity), with lower-income and less-educated parents tending to feel less sure that they had the information they needed. Although the majority of parents of children with severe or profound needs also felt they had the information they needed, larger numbers of these parents felt they did not have all the information they needed. By comparison, Teske et al. found that nearly 20 percent of parents of students in general education felt they were missing information.[56]

What Are the Decisionmaking Processes?

In theory, choice is rational and data driven; in practice, serendipity seems to play a role. Despite the arduous process many parents went through to find the right fit for their child, some expressed the feeling that finding the right school was a matter of "blind luck." Parents talked about services that were promised but not delivered, and the need to constantly monitor their child's education to ensure that the right school continued to be the right school. One parent described an exhaustive research process that nonetheless resulted in enrolling her child in a school that seemed wonderful, but turned out to be disastrous. On the other hand, another parent found her child's school by accidentally entering the wrong building.

Faced with an overwhelming amount of information and an inability to know the future, human beings often "satisfice" by selecting options that are "good enough" rather than perfect.[57] This seems to apply to parental decisionmaking as well. For example, Teske et al. suggest that low-income parents effectively use information to find several schools that are "good enough" in terms of meeting their child's needs, and then pick what they perceive to be the best one.[58]

There are several ways in which the decisionmaking process of parents of children with special needs seems to differ somewhat from the processes of other parents. First, special education parents generally believe that what will be "good enough" for a typical student may well not be good enough for their children, and that this mismatch could have devastating implications for their

---

56. Ibid.
57. Simon, 1976.
58. Teske, Fitzpatrick, and Kaplan, 2007.

sons and daughters. These parents are looking for schools that *will* meet their children's specific needs. At the same time, these parents have a sense that there is no school that will always meet all of their child's specific needs. There is an understanding that they will need to monitor the school closely and be prepared to move again if the school does not work out as hoped. As a result, the decisionmaking does not end with the selection of a particular school. As one parent put it: "You won't find the perfect school, so you have to find the best possible and then work with what you have."

Are Charter Schools Perceived as Viable Options?

As noted above, concern has been expressed about the ability of charter schools to meet the needs of special education students. The concern may stem from financial issues or concerns about staff competence and knowledge. However, we found no evidence of this concern in the focus groups or surveys. These parents in Denver and Milwaukee seemed to consider charter schools as part of the greater universe of schools that might, or might not, be able to meet the needs of their children. The designation of a school as a charter school, traditional public school, or private school did not by itself direct the searches of most parents. This is understandable in light of the wide variety of children's needs and instructional approaches required to meet them.

Contrary to past findings, we did not see strong indications that parents were "fleeing" from traditional public schools to charter schools because of a specific opinion about the nature of traditional public schools versus the nature of charter schools. While the survey results did show that most current charter school parents who had changed schools had previously attended traditional public schools, there was a wide variety of "switching" going on. With that said, parents in Denver were noticeably unhappier with the district's approach to special education.

Focus group conversations revealed that parents seemed to be quite willing to change schools in any direction, guided more by their children's specific needs than by the label attached to a school. Parents who had left other schools reported issues with safety and special education services in both charter and traditional public schools. In making their decision, parents currently in charter schools reported also looking at traditional public schools, and vice versa. Some traditional public school parents also reported looking at traditional public

"They don't advertise as a high-needs school, but it is known."
—*Milwaukee parent in traditional school*

schools in nearby districts that had positive reputations for special education services (although parents in both Milwaukee and Denver reported that other districts were highly reluctant to accept out-of-district special education students). The districts studied have long-term experience with charter schools and school choice, so that parents may be used to charter schools as simply an option, rather than viewing charter schools *per se* as a new answer to the challenges they face.

We did not find that parents were counseled away from charter schools on a regular basis. We found that some parents were on occasion counseled away from particular schools. Thirteen percent of survey respondents reported this had happened to them. This did not seem to be limited to charter schools; in fact, most of these parents reported being counseled away from traditional public schools. This seemed to happen a lot to parents of autistic children. In general, parents did not perceive an unwillingness of charter schools to serve their children as compared with other types of schools. In fact, some charter schools enjoy an informal reputation among parent networks as providing a haven for special education students, as do some neighborhood schools.

Why Choose Charter or Traditional Public Schools?

Survey respondents were asked why they chose their current school (whether charter or traditional). Each of the following reasons was cited by one-third or more of the parents:
- Safe: 78 percent
- Curriculum/instructional approach: 76 percent
- Reputation of school: 71 percent
- Special education services: 70 percent
- Better fit for child: 69 percent
- Small class size: 69 percent
- Individualized attention: 68 percent
- Staff qualifications: 67 percent
- School philosophy: 58 percent
- Convenient location: 55 percent
- Teacher child likes: 54 percent
- Referred to school: 43 percent
- Child wanted to attend: 35 percent

School safety, curriculum and instructional approach, the reputation of the school, and availability of special education services top the list. Some of these items may be different ways of commenting on the same thing (e.g., school safety and reputation of the school). It is interesting that a battery of responses revolving around school quality and instructional program elicit support from two-thirds or more of the respondents (staff qualifications, individualized attention, class size, "fit," and reputation of the school). Lower-income parents were more likely to mention safety as a key factor, probably reflecting the neighborhoods in which they live. Interestingly, they also paid more attention to special education services. Higher-income parents were more likely to mention smaller class size and school curriculum/instructional approach.

Although for the most part parents seemed to view charters as part of a wide array of possible choices, some parents did mention what they felt to be specific benefits of charter schools compared to traditional public schools. Others mentioned school characteristics that are often thought of as more likely to be present in a charter school setting.

For example, many parents mentioned that they appreciated the way in which their children were included in the regular classroom at charter schools. At many traditional public schools, children with special needs are "pulled out" to work in resource rooms or other self-contained classrooms for part of the day. This can be very stigmatizing to children, especially those with less visible disabilities who keenly want to fit in. One Milwaukee parent described appreciation for the inclusive nature of her child's charter school because "they aren't made to feel stupid by going to dumb class."

Some charter schools appear to be using resources and setting up classrooms in ways that minimize the need for pullouts. Instead, the special education needs of individual children are met within the classroom, either through instructional techniques or staffing that occurs within the classroom. Some parents mentioned that charter schools have flexibility to "finagle" resources to put more teachers in the classroom, which leads to smaller student-teacher ratios and greater opportunities for individualized instruction. Other charter schools have instructional approaches that allow for fluid groupings of children, another way to meet individual needs. However, parents also mentioned traditional public schools that offer similar benefits, such as the state-funded SAGE classrooms in Milwaukee, which offer a 15:1 student-teacher ratio.[59]

How Do Mild Versus Severe Needs of Students Affect Parent Choice?

It is also important here to distinguish between the instructional needs of children with mild/moderate disabilities and those with more severe disabilities. Some children will benefit hugely from being able to stay in a regular classroom, and their parents make choices based on that benefit. However, other children have levels of disability that benefit much more from instruction in a

---

59. The SAGE program, however, is an example of the ways in which even a simple student-teacher ratio can be perceived very differently by parents. Parents reported that in some cases, schools were complying with the SAGE ratio by simply inserting more teachers into large classrooms, an approach that will not benefit students who have difficulties with auditory or sensory processing issues, for example.

self-contained resource room, surrounded by peers of like ability. As a result, what one parent looks for in an instructional setting will be the opposite of what another parent looks for.

Consistent with this theory, respondents in our survey who had children with more severe special needs tended to be in traditional public schools, which are more likely to provide a self-contained classroom approach. This was consistent with the national results found by T. A. Fiore.[60] Overall our survey results indicated that 15 percent of the children had severe or profound disabilities, and these children represented 30 percent of respondents in traditional public schools. Meanwhile, nearly 90 percent of the charter school respondents reported that their students' disabilities were mild or moderate. For parents of students with less severe needs, the flexibility and individualized nature of some charter classrooms can provide benefits on par with more formal interventions written into an individualized education program (IEP).

Are Charter Schools More Different than Alike?

Charter schools themselves differ from school to school. At least one charter school in both districts had been or was being established specifically to enroll children with severe needs. In some charter schools, classroom sizes are too large to satisfy parents that their children will receive individualized attention. A focus on rigorous academics at some charters is appealing to some parents, who feel their children's abilities are being unfairly discounted, but unappealing to others, whose children may get left behind very quickly in that type of environment. Other charter schools were criticized for being "too loose" or failing to use report cards.

We asked charter school survey respondents whether their school had a specific instructional program or curricular approach that brought them to the school. A large number of parents did not answer this question, perhaps indicating unfamiliarity with these specialized terms. Of those who did answer the question, 55 percent reported that such factors did bring them to the school, while 23 percent answered in the negative and 22 percent reported that they did not know. Parents were invited to write in the program or curriculum that brought them to the school, producing a wide variety of responses. Some parents chose their schools because of special education emphasis and/or experience; others chose a college preparatory curriculum or a math- and science-focused school. Some parents were very clear about the approach used by the school, mentioning specific reading programs or curricula by name; others simply reported that their school was "a school where kids learn different" or "ayudan mas mejor" ("they help better").

---

60. Fiore, 2000.

Nearly one-quarter of charter school respondents reported that their school served primarily special-needs children. When we compared this result to the actual list of schools attended, it appears that either parents are mistaken or that some of these schools have in fact developed significant special education populations through these "word-of-mouth" networks.

Family convenience factors (such as transportation and the location of other siblings' schools) were often mentioned by parents as factoring into their decisions; however these were paramount factors for only a few parents. The majority of survey respondents reported that transportation issues did not influence their choice of schools. Many of these children could be eligible for district-provided transportation as part of an IEP, but parents in focus groups expressed concern about the ability of their children to safely use even supervised transportation. Parents generally provided transportation for their children, although greater numbers of low-income parents relied on school buses.

Why Stay at a Particular School or Leave It?

One striking characteristic of school choice for parents of students with special needs is the ongoing nature of their decisionmaking process. These parents not only pay a lot of attention when they select a school initially, they are also continuously engaged in monitoring the services provided while advocating for their children after the school is selected. If a school is not working out as expected, these parents often will pull up stakes and leave.

We asked survey respondents whose children had previously attended other schools for the reasons why they left those schools. About one-quarter cited reasons having little to do with satisfaction or dissatisfaction with the school, such as moving or grade transitions (e.g., moving from an elementary school to a middle school). However, the majority reported being dissatisfied with one or more aspects of the prior school:

- The school was not a good fit: 48 percent
- Dissatisfied with teacher: 45 percent
- Child was struggling academically: 43 percent
- School didn't communicate: 42 percent
- Dissatisfied with special education services: 39 percent
- Child needed fresh start: 32 percent
- Class sizes too large: 31 percent
- School was unsafe: 30 percent
- Too far away: 12 percent
- No transportation was available: 11 percent
- Unable to take child to school: 4 percent

In focus groups, parents who were unhappy reported the sense of being in a constant battle with the school to receive services mandated by their child's IEP. The most notable difficulty parents had was getting a paraprofessional or classroom aide to be with their child. Schools would often promise a classroom aide and then either not provide one at all, or divide up the aide's time among several children. Some parents had solved this problem by simply paying a classroom aide out of their own pocket to be with their child full-time. This sense of frustration was most notable in Denver, although it was also mentioned in Milwaukee.

In general, parents reported being satisfied with the special education services their children received at their current schools. Eighty-one percent of survey respondents reported that they were "very" or "somewhat" satisfied with special education services at their current schools. Just six percent reported being "very" or "somewhat" dissatisfied. Eighty-four percent of parents reported that they were "very" or "somewhat" satisfied with how their school's staff and teachers communicate and work with them. Again, these numbers are consistent with national results.[61]

Parents in focus groups viewed the school principal as key to establishing a culture that served special-needs families. Schools that received high praise were described as open and welcoming, with staff that were responsive to families and communicated with them regularly and well. Spanish-speaking parents also were pleased with programs that helped them understand how they could help their children. A good principal was seen as essential to setting this type of tone at a school.

Other parents reported that the combination of a "good" IEP and a school that would work with them in delivering the services mandated under the IEP made for a positive school experience. These parents were well aware that the IEP was a powerful tool in their hands as they advocated for their children; however, whether the intentions of the IEP would come to fruition at a particular school depended on the willingness of the school staff to meet their child's needs. Other parents did not appear as cognizant of their legal rights to enforce the IEP.

CONCLUSION

Despite the difficulties inherent in maneuvering legal and financial special education requirements within an autonomous school structure, charter schools do seem to be viable options for a large number of families with students with special needs. In fact, some charter schools have developed informal reputations as havens for students with special needs. In many cases, particularly with respect

---

61. Newman, 2005; Johnson and Duffett, 2002.

to the needs of students with less severe disabilities, the variety of instructional approaches offered by charter schools can serve as beneficial interventions for these students. Effective inclusion for students with less severe needs seems to be a particular strength of many charter schools.

The parents of children with special needs look very much like parents of typical children in the information sources they use to engage in school choice decisions. However, parents of children with special needs view them as fragile and susceptible to greater damage if the wrong school is chosen. As a result, the school choice process seems to be even more focused on the needs of the individual child, and parents continue to monitor the school closely to make sure that initial expectations and ongoing needs are met. Parents feel that no one will advocate for their child as strongly as they will. They also understand that the needs of their child and the financial pressures experienced by schools and districts are often at odds. This is exhausting and frustrating for many parents.

Because of the highly individualized nature of this process, differences across schools (whether traditional or charter) seem to be more important to the parents of children with special needs than are more general differences between charter schools and traditional public schools. Whether they attend charter schools or traditional public schools, parents want schools that accept and care about their children, that both challenge and support their children, and that work with parents as active and respected partners in the ongoing education of their children.

Chapter 4

Case Studies of Charter Innovation and Success

Lauren Morando Rhim, Dana Brinson, and Joanne Jacobs

Ideally, charter developers use their autonomy to develop new, robust educational options for all children, including students with special needs. This chapter presents findings from case studies of six charter schools identified by leading special educators and charter experts as programs successfully educating children with disabilities.[62] The case studies are exploratory in nature. They document the innovative or successful components of the special education services provided by these six schools.

The six schools are located in different states, each with its own distinctive policy environment. Although each school is unique in its approach, collectively they provide insight into practices that hold promise for educating children with disabilities in both traditional and charter public schools. This chapter presents descriptions of the individual case study schools. A cross-case analysis is presented in chapter 5.

SELECTION PROCESS

To identify the six schools, we sought nominations from experts with knowledge of the charter sector or special education. Our selection criteria were academic achievement, special education enrollment, innovative or promising

Case Study Schools

- Charyl Stockwell Academy, Howell, Michigan
- CHIME Arnold Schwarzenegger Charter Elementary and Middle Schools, Woodland Hills, California
- ISUS Institute of Construction Technology, Dayton, Ohio
- Metro Deaf School, St. Paul, Minnesota
- Roxbury Preparatory Charter School, Boston, Massachusetts
- Woodland Elementary Charter School, Atlanta, Georgia

---

62. The full case studies for each of these schools can be found in Rhim and Brinson, 2008.

practices, and diversity of schools according to multiple characteristics such as student demographics and policy environment. Using these criteria, we identified an initial pool of 33 schools and subsequently selected 6 schools based on the degree to which they reflected the criteria.

We conducted daylong school visits between December 2007 and February 2008. During the site visits, we toured the schools and interviewed a minimum of three people. We also reviewed multiple documents for each school (e.g., annual reports, renewal applications, and school report cards) and school websites. To verify data, we triangulated data collected via interviews with multiple informants and our document reviews. Based on the interviews and document reviews, we developed individual school case studies, which we then analyzed to identify recurring characteristics and practices.

THE SCHOOLS

In chapter 5, we outline 4 broad characteristics and 12 related practices that appear to be linked to these schools' successes. While these characteristics and practices are noteworthy from a policy perspective, equally noteworthy from the perspective of educators and parents are the schools themselves. We describe each of them briefly below before turning to a discussion of commonalities across schools.

The programs described range from those serving students with relatively mild learning disabilities to those educating students with more severe challenges, including autism and Down syndrome. The schools, located from California through the Midwest to New England, serve students from kindergarten through high school. The programs emphasize school teamwork, mission, and student inclusion. In short, they emphasize the very things promoted by the Individuals with Disabilities Education Act (IDEA).

Charyl Stockwell Academy

Experienced special educators Chuck and Shelley Stockwell founded Livingston Developmental Academy in Michigan in 1996 to provide a safe, enriching charter school focused on reducing early learning failure and, ultimately, decreasing the number of students identified for special education. After years working as administrators and teachers, the Stockwells had become disillusioned with the changes made in special education. Under the auspices of inclusion, schools reduced the services provided to students with the most severe disabilities and greatly increased the number of students identified under the broad category of "specific learning disabilities." This process, Chuck Stockwell lamented, "created a whole new group of special education children to get thrown away."

Worst of all, the Stockwells believed, the increase in special education interventions were not resulting in improved learning outcomes.

The Stockwells knew there had to be a better way, and their professional concerns were reinforced when their daughter Charyl was diagnosed with a brain tumor that affected her learning abilities. The lack of answers they received from educational specialists about their daughter's learning needs strengthened the Stockwells' resolve to improve approaches to special education.

Livingston Developmental Academy (renamed the Charyl Stockwell Academy [CSA] when their daughter passed away in 2001) employs an intensive approach that evaluates every child's skills and provides multi-age learning "families" in which students can develop at their own pace. CSA's educational approach centers on full inclusion and the belief that early intervention and excellent teaching can prevent many children from being diagnosed as having a disability. While schools often label 12 to 15 percent of students as disabled, the Stockwells believe only 3 to 4 percent have disabilities that cannot easily be addressed in the general classroom environment. Chuck Stockwell noted, "Not all five-year-olds belong in kindergarten, or six-year-olds in first grade. Kids who don't meet that schedule we call 'learning disabled' or 'emotionally impaired' or 'cognitively impaired.' The difference between a kid with a 100 IQ and one with a 75 IQ is that the kid with the 75 needs more time to learn." Shelly Stockwell concurred, saying, "And all children have asynchronous development. A seven-year-old child might be ten intellectually and six emotionally."

At CSA, two teachers work with a group of 40 students across two grade levels. Team teaching allows students to be grouped by performance level in various subjects without being segregated. Students in kindergarten through third grade and new students are screened for developmental issues associated with acquisition of gross and fine motor skills; sensory integration; self-control; ability to focus; as well as auditory, visual, and language problems. Supplementing the team-teaching model, trained aides provide "sensory breaks" for students who get overwhelmed in class. An aide takes the child out of the room to run around the gym, do deep breathing exercises, or do heavy lifting to work off excess energy and calm down. Rather than provide a single resource teacher to a single child, this model provides targeted supports when students need them and removes those supports when they do not. CSA's intervention-driven approach actually employs fewer special educators and resource aides than other special education models.

Children who fall behind academically are referred to a Teacher Support Team (TST), which analyzes why the child is struggling and comes up with strategies. Unlike the resource-room model where students are provided general tutoring or other help, TST is "very clear and focused," Shelley Stockwell noted. "It's intense. If there's no progress, we change the program." The team profiles the child's health history and family issues in order to learn why academics are suffering. Does he sleep through the night? What does he eat? "We assess and intervene, assess and intervene, assess and intervene," Chuck Stockwell explained. "Intervention is based on a theory of what's going on."

Although parents in the area have many high-performing schools to choose from, the Stockwell charter school has found it easy to attract students. Parents like the small classes, individual attention, and the promise that children will progress at their own pace. The school's character education program, which helps students develop self-control, is another draw.

About 8 percent of CSA students receive special education services, though many more likely qualified at one time. During the 2006–07 school year, 12 of the 70 students identified for special education met their individualized education program (IEP) goals and no longer qualified for special education. On average, CSA students with disabilities gain 1.2 grades per year in English and 1.6 per year in math, often allowing them to close any learning gap with their typically developing peers by the 8th grade. The approach works and teachers must buy in to the school's approach or go elsewhere, said Chuck. "You're not coming here to do your own thing. We're a vision-driven school. We don't believe in academic freedom. We believe in mission."

CHIME Arnold Schwarzenegger Charter Elementary and Middle Schools

The CHIME Institute's Elementary and Middle Charter schools are small schools located outside of Los Angeles and are part of Los Angeles Unified School District. We chose to include CHIME in our case studies due to its success educating students with a wide range of disabilities in a remarkably inclusive setting. At CHIME, general and special education teachers work as partners to support all students. This co-teaching model, intensive classroom support, regular teacher planning, and a constructivist instructional model all seem to contribute to the school's academic results.

All CHIME students have individual learning plans. In 2007, approximately 20 percent of the school's students were diagnosed with a disability that qualified them for special education, including children with severe disabilities. The elementary school met adequate yearly progress (AYP) targets in 2005, 2006, and 2007; the middle school has met AYP in 2005 and 2006.

CHIME Institute was started as a model demonstration project funded for three years (1987–90) by the U.S. Department of Education. Originally, it was known as the Children's Center Handicapped Integration Model Educational (CCHIME) Project. Its goal was to develop an effective model for providing special educational services at an existing child development program, housed at California State University, Northridge (CSUN).

Claire Cavallaro and Michele Haney, professors in the special education program at the CSUN College of Education, established the CHIME Institute as a private nonprofit corporation in August 1990, to continue and extend the work of the earlier grant. The CHIME Charter Elementary School was established in fall 2001 and serves children from kindergarten through 5th grade. The CHIME Charter Middle School opened fall 2003, serving students in 6th to 8th grade in fall 2004. In 2007, the elementary school was named in honor of California's governor and his commitment to education.

Students at CHIME can be seen using walkers at recess and communications devices in class, and some children leave class to jump on a mini-trampoline set outside the door. While we were visiting, an aide was using flash cards, a tape player, and a stoplight timer to work with a first grader with Down syndrome, while his classmates discussed a story they had read.

What is interesting about these scenes is that they are accepted so matter-of-factly at CHIME. Children do not point or tease. They do not seem to notice "difference" or ability versus disability. At CHIME, students are accustomed to differences. CHIME uses an old elementary school site in an affluent, leafy neighborhood. But the students come from many different San Fernando Valley communities representing 32 different zip codes. In 2007, about half the students were white, one-third Hispanic, and the rest black or Asian American.

Co-teaching makes inclusion work. It really is all about teamwork. There is no such thing as a lonely teacher at the school. Special educators and paraprofessionals are in general education classrooms working with students with disabilities—and with other children who need help that day. Nobody is pulled out. After classes end, teachers, special educators, and aides meet in grade level teams for 25 minutes to "debrief." All are considered part of the teaching team.

The school does not wait for students to get behind before offering extra help. A language-and-speech pathologist and a recreational therapist work with kindergartners at risk for reading problems. "We went from 15 at-risk kindergartners to 2," said Principal Julie Fabrocini, reflecting on the value of the therapists to early intervention. With help with phonological awareness, language, and speech, most will do well in 1st grade.

The teachers make sure students know what is expected. Teaching behavioral expectations explicitly helps children on the autism spectrum—and everyone else. Classes include students who are gifted, typical, low-achievers, and disabled. Co-teaching, co-planning, and co-assessing make inclusion work, said teacher Rachel Knopf.

It is hard to find schools with so much commitment to making inclusion work. One parent of a child with cerebral palsy said she feels she is part of a team with everyone working on the same goal. "There's so much understanding and openness," she observed. For example, when one student—a boy with autism and a lot of excess energy—feels himself losing control, he walks outside, jumps on a small trampoline set up for him and then runs around. When he is calmed down, he returns to class. At his previous school, Fabrocini noted, an aide held him down when he could not sit still.

The mother of a second grader without a disability said she chose CHIME over other local schools because of its small size and its strong mission: "Everybody is here and everybody is welcome." She believes her son will learn life skills at the school that he would not learn in a more conventional environment with less diversity in terms of learning styles and abilities. Her son told her that he wished one of his friends would talk more but said they enjoyed painting together. She found out later the friend is unable to talk. Her son had not mentioned that the older boy had a disability.

ISUS Institute of Construction Technology

Improved Solutions for Urban Systems (ISUS) schools in Dayton, Ohio, provide dropout recovery services and help students develop marketable skills in growth industries. Founder Ann Higdon responded to Dayton's drop-out crisis and the growing pressures that unemployed and court-involved young people placed on the city's budget by providing a place where teens could learn to transcend their challenges and develop into self-sufficient young adults. Most ISUS students have dropped out of their first high school or stopped going to class; 80 percent have been involved with the juvenile justice system. As with most drop-out populations, students with disabilities are overrepresented. In 2007, about 27 percent of ISUS's students had a diagnosed disability; nearly all were behind in reading, writing, and math skills.

At ISUS's Construction Institute, students work toward graduation while developing vocational skills they will need for jobs in construction, such as dry walling or heavy equipment operation. At the same time, students receive individual counseling, life skills development, job search support, college placement services, and assistance with any family challenges they may have. The program meets students where they are, and provides them with tailored pathways to graduation and employment. At the start and end of each school day, students, teachers, and administrators gather for a "family meeting" to resolve problems and discuss issues. ISUS assumes every student has special needs, not just those who enter with an IEP. This individualized environment supports all students, those with and without a disability.

When students first come to ISUS, they meet with a life skills coach and a counselor. Some have been out of school for years and some have their own children to raise. At ISUS, every student's goal is to pass the Ohio Graduation Tests in reading, writing, math, science, and social studies. It is not easy. "Most students, regardless of disability status, enter at age 16 or older with first- through fourth-grade reading skills," said Sally Gordon, the intervention specialist. "For example, I've had a 16-year-old boy who only knew five letters and two or three sounds when he came to this school." Every ISUS teacher has been trained in the Wilson reading program to remediate students with such low reading skills.

ISUS also provides its students with disabilities with a series of push-in and pull-out services directly aligned with IEP goals. Malaika Dedrick, the special education director, reported that special education works at ISUS because she helps all teachers embrace their responsibilities for educating students with disabilities and ensures students receiving special education services are not singled out or seen as different. This approach apparently works because, as one student noted, "We all need extra help, that's why we're here."

Once students have demonstrated commitment to the program and academic progress, they also begin working "on site." While building houses, students develop construction skills, make money, and can earn industry-recognized certifications.

At the time of this study, Construction Institute students had built 30 houses in one Dayton community since 2002 and had plans to build 30 more. Already, ISUS homes have turned around a neighborhood near the University of Dayton, reported founder Higdon. "Our kids were the first to hammer a nail there. It was a ghost town."

The direct relationship between what students are learning—in the classroom and on the construction site—to their future as adults provides youth with a reason to come to, and engage with, school. And the Construction Institute serves just 120 students at a time, so getting lost is not an option. When they are building houses, students reinforce their academic skills through activities such as reading directions and using math to determine how many cubic yards of concrete they need for a project.

One student, who was diagnosed with a learning disability in elementary school, says he chose ISUS to better himself. He finds it easier to learn at ISUS where classes are quiet, there are few distractions, and he feels more motivated. "You're not just sitting in a classroom reading about something, you're actually doing something with what you're learning. You can read 10 books but it's not like doing it."

Higdon attributes ISUS's success with serving students with disabilities to the combination of intensive social and emotional supports and the pride developed while students (1) develop work skills, (2) work toward a high school diploma, and (3) acquire industry certifications. ISUS can enforce rules because students understand that the rules of the school are linked to the rules of work. "Here if you cut school, they tell your parents right away," said one student. "I think they've got their own mailman running back and forth to students'

homes: 'Your kid didn't come to school today!' Your parents are going to know!"
"Somebody actually cares," another student said. "They care about your educa-
tion. If they want you to have an education that much, then how much should
I want my education? "

Metro Deaf School

Metro Deaf School (MDS) in St. Paul, Minnesota, typically serves students who
are deaf and hard of hearing. Director Dyan Sherwood co-founded MDS in 1993
to continue a dual-language American Sign Language (ASL)/written English
program she had been piloting in St. Paul Public Schools for two years. All MDS
students qualify for special education.

After twenty years as a teacher of the deaf and hard of hearing (D/HH) population in the district's self-contained classrooms, Sherwood and a group of committed parents and teachers grasped the new charter school opportunity and
opened a school focused solely on D/HH education through a dual-language
approach. Sherwood had grown frustrated with schools trying to "be all things
to all people." She had experienced the fractured environment of deaf classrooms where teachers employed a variety of approaches to deaf education—
including ASL, cued speech, lip reading, oral/aural, or other approaches—in an
attempt to use each method requested by parents. Sherwood noted that the
results of these efforts were confused classrooms, poor language development,
missed opportunities for social and emotional development, and no access to
role models who are deaf.

Because MDS serves students with a low-incidence disability, the school has
remained small.[63] Their renovated school building can comfortably hold 100
students, but the average student population is 60. In addition to a small number of new prekindergarten students joining MDS each year, school administrators have found that there is a large influx of 4th or 5th graders who have
attended their district schools and have not been successful with an interpreter
or with cochlear implants.[64] Director Sherwood recalled from her 35 years in
deaf education that many deaf students around the age of 10 begin to advocate

---

63. Nationally, students who are deaf or hearing impaired represent approximately 1 percent of the
school-age population. U.S. Department of Education, Office of Special Education and Rehabilitative
Services, Office of Special Education Programs, 2009.

64. Cochlear implants are small electronic devices that are surgically placed inside an individual's ear
to help them hear sound. The device does not restore hearing but can help a person who is profoundly
deaf or hard of hearing to hear sounds, which can help them understand language. Use of the implants
requires therapy to teach the individual how to use the sound they hear. "Cochlear Implants," National
Institute on Deafness and Other Communication Disorders, http://www.nidcd.nih.gov/health/hearing/
coch.asp.

for themselves, seek to be around other kids who are deaf or hard of hearing, and want to learn to communicate more effectively with them.

The school aims to provide an academically rigorous, socially supportive, and engaging environment. Teachers provide instruction in math, language arts, science, and art to all students. During one science lesson, for instance, a teacher was introducing vocabulary for and concepts of electric motors. The teacher had parts of a small electrical motor, including battery, wire, and a switch. As he held up the parts for the students to see, he signed the appropriate ASL sign and then held up a card with the written English word for each part.

To evaluate academic progress, MDS's students participate in the state standardized tests designed for their non-disabled, English-speaking peers. Despite challenges associated with administering tests designed for hearing children, 37 percent of MDS students performed proficiently or better on the exams in 2007. School personnel reported that student performance on standardized tests varies widely and they attributed the variability to two factors: (1) the routine influx of students during the 4th and 5th grades who arrive with poorly developed language skills, and (2) many students with dual or multiple disabilities including blindness, autism, or developmental cognitive delays that hamper their academic progress. Sherwood argued that, "If there aren't other complicating factors, the kids can be on grade level if given access to a language—ASL—early."

To support the development of the whole child, MDS hires occupational and physical therapists, speech clinicians, a social worker, and a clinical psychologist. Several of these specialists are deaf, providing both valuable services and access to deaf role models for MDS students. Throughout the school, MDS personnel provide not only access to language and individualized education, but seek to develop in their students social skills, acceptance of differences, and empathy for peers. These efforts at building an inclusive environment help MDS effectively serve all of its students, who range from academically gifted to having profound cognitive delays.

Director Sherwood acknowledged the controversies surrounding special education and schools serving only students with disabilities. Some argue that schools like MDS segregate students with disabilities from their non-disabled peers. Sherwood believes that what is most important is for a single approach to be implemented throughout a deaf education program because her experience has shown her that it facilitates communication between students, the development of social skills, and improved academic performance. Such a singularly focused approach to deaf education was not possible in the comprehensive district schools, but is possible at her school and others in the area. She pointed out that there was a good program for the deaf a half-hour from St. Paul that devoted its program to the cued speech approach. When she receives an application from a parent who wants his or her child to be taught to use cued speech, Sherwood refers the parent to the other school. These schools provide choice to parents while providing a coherent, unified approach to education for D/HH students.

A mother who is deaf explained that having the opportunity to have her two children, who are also deaf, educated in their first language at MDS is one of the primary reasons she chose the school. "I firmly believe that ASL is their foundation language," and she noted that in a traditional public school," [If] you were the only deaf child, I don't believe you would have as many opportunities as the kids do here." For her, MDS is the least-restrictive environment available, and she believes her children are thriving as a result.

Roxbury Preparatory Charter School

Boston's Roxbury Preparatory Charter School serves grades 6 through 8 and focuses on preparing its students to enter, succeed in, and graduate from college. Roxbury Prep was founded on the philosophy that all students are entitled to and can succeed in college preparatory programs when (1) the curriculum is rigorous, engaging, and well-planned; (2) the school emphasizes student character, community responsibility, and exposure to life's possibilities; and (3) a community network supports student academic, social, and physical well-being.

Though Roxbury Prep is a middle school, it offers support to students all the way through high school and college. Two full-time coordinators help students apply to college prep high schools, apply for internships during high school, make weekly phone calls to graduates, and provide weekend workshops on college preparatory topics. They then go on to provide similar types of assistance as students apply to college. The intensive, long-term support provided by the school is especially helpful for students at Roxbury who qualify for special education (about 12 percent of all students in 2008). As of fall 2008, one hundred percent of Roxbury Prep's students had been accepted to college prep high schools and 87 percent of their graduates had enrolled in some form of post-secondary education.

At Roxbury Prep, most students do not know who has an IEP and is entitled to special education services and who is not. Everyone is included in the classroom and many students who do not have IEPs nonetheless get extra help. "The reason why our special education program is successful is because our regular education is successful," said co-director Dana Lehman. "A lot of special ed is a way to get kids who are hard to serve away from teachers who don't want to serve them," Lehman believes. They counter that trend at Roxbury Prep by reinforcing with all teachers that they are responsible for teaching every student.

The general classroom environment at Roxbury Prep is also conducive to serving students with disabilities. "Many of the accommodations typical of IEPs are simply standard procedure at our school," noted individual needs coordinator Jamie Thornton. The school's philosophy is that all students benefit from structure, monitoring, clear and repeated directions, and work that is broken into learnable chunks. Many students who may have had IEPs at another school no longer need them once they come to Roxbury Prep because of the supports provided in the classroom.

The school uses pre- and post-tests for each class and routine interim assessments throughout the year to develop highly individualized educational programs for all students. Because most students enter Roxbury Prep one or more grade levels behind, the school provides intensive evaluation to tailor teaching to the areas of greatest need. In addition, Roxbury Prep provides practice testing for various standardized and entrance exams to college preparatory high schools to preemptively identify shortfalls and aid teachers in providing any necessary remedial supports. Roxbury Prep employs two special educators who spend more than 60 percent of their time providing push-in services in the general education classroom. While in the classroom, special educators help other students, not only students with IEPs. This "normalization" of individualized education appears to facilitate access to the general education curriculum and academic success for students with disabilities.

Some students—with and without disabilities—find the school's academic expectations too demanding and choose to leave. Because of the college focus and rigorous academic program, Roxbury Prep typically serves students with mild to moderate learning disabilities. Parents of students with more severe disabilities have not generally chosen to enroll their child in Roxbury Prep. For those who do enroll and stay on, the school has proven that students with disabilities can rise to the challenge of a college-bound vision. "We had a girl who was in my office all the time complaining the work was too hard," said Jenna Leary, the learning specialist. "Now she's in high school calling me to complain it's too easy. She wants me to get her into honor classes."

One mother of a student with disabilities enthusiastically shared the story of her son who has only been at Roxbury Prep for a few months. At his previous school, his reading and writing grades were C's, she recalls. At Roxbury Prep, he now earns A's and B's. She credits this change to the dedication of the school personnel. She said, regarding her requests for help and support for her son, "They never say to me, 'No.' They always say, 'That's OK, we can do that.'" This mother also appreciates more than the academic program, saying, "This is my second family here. My son is so happy."

An enduring reflection of Roxbury Prep's impact on students with disabilities is perhaps evident in the later success of their graduates. Of the four students who had IEPs while attending Roxbury Prep and are now college age, all four graduated high school and were accepted to college.

Woodland Elementary Charter School

Woodland Elementary Charter School is a large, comprehensive elementary school that converted to charter status in 2001. It was the first public school to convert in Fulton County School District, a suburb of Atlanta. In 2006, the school successfully renewed its charter based on demonstrating that it had attained multiple academic performance goals and outperformed comparable schools in the district.

Seven years after converting to charter status, the school enrolled over 800 students, including a preschool and school-age program for children with moderate, severe, and profound disabilities, as well as a Talented-and-Gifted (TAG) program. The school was also ethnically, linguistically, and economically diverse.

In 2007, approximately 12 percent of the students at Woodland had a disability that qualified them for special education and related services. This figure includes children enrolled in the prekindergarten center-based program for children and the center-based programs for school-age children. The charter school operates as part of the district and, in line with state charter policy, the school provides the district with copies of all IEPs, uses school district transportation, and the district provides related services when required. Special education costs are largely drawn from their per-pupil allocation provided by the district.

The school has used the autonomy under its charter to alter the allocation of existing per-pupil funds to support the implementation of the Schoolwide Enrichment Model developed in the 1970s by Joseph Renzulli.[65] Among other features, Woodland has a science lab, operates a planetarium in the building, offers a Suzuki violin program to all students, requires students to wear uniforms, and maintains a mandatory parental participation policy. The school also operates a school-within-a-school for children experiencing emotional or behavioral problems that impact their academic progress.

Woodland Elementary was selected for case study due to the proportionate percentage of students receiving special education services relative to the district

---

65. According to the Neag Center for Gifted Education and Talent Development at the University of Connecticut: "The Schoolwide Enrichment Model (SEM) is a detailed blueprint for total school improvement that allows each school the flexibility to develop its own unique programs based on local resources, student demographics, and school dynamics as well as faculty strengths and creativity. Although this research-based model is based on highly successful practices that originated in special programs for the gifted and talented students, its major goal is to promote both challenging and enjoyable high-end learning across a wide range of school types, levels and demographic differences." For more information, see: http://www.gifted.uconn.edu/sem/semexec.html.

average *and* in light of academic outcomes for students with disabilities that exceed local averages. In spring 2007, 64 percent of the students with disabilities districtwide met or exceeded the state standard in math, whereas 88 percent of the students with disabilities at Woodland met or exceeded standards.

Woodland is a large school and maintains a staff of approximately 130 instructional personnel and support staff. The school also employs a resource teacher for every grade level and the local district provides related services personnel as requested. The school's charter explicitly excludes the school from district involuntary school transfer policies. Reflecting their commitment to training all teachers in TAG instructional strategies, the school's renewal application notes: "Our charter requires very unique training needs and long-term commitments on the part of our teachers and we need, therefore, to be very selective about our teachers and their placement to insure success."

Principal Ruth Baskerville explained that teachers are required to complete a nine-week gifted education instruction strategies training class. In addition, Woodland employs cluster TAG teachers (i.e., teachers with a gifted education endorsement) at each grade level. The school uses the funds allocated to hire a full-time TAG teacher to instead hire a gifted-endorsed teacher to provide ongoing training to all teachers in TAG teaching strategies. She explained that rather than using the full-time equivalent teacher "to benefit some kids, it benefits all kids."

Both teachers and administrators recalled stories of children with disabilities responding well to TAG instructional strategies and, in some instances, surprising their teachers with their abilities. TAG liaison Anita Lindsley noted: "I am blown away by what my kids [with disabilities] say. [The approach] did not require rote memory. It is not that type of baseline thinking. There is more than one right answer. For their self-esteem, it is beautiful . . . . They will come up with the response and, wow, the teacher realizes they could have missed out on that kind of teaching for a child."

The school also practices looping, wherein classroom teachers rise with their students in two-year cycles. According to the school's renewal application, with looping "the quality of learning time is increased because students and teachers do not experience discontinuity and separation commonly found in the straight-grade class; and students transfer both content and class-management knowledge to a higher degree. In addition, having cohort groups of students for multiple years reportedly facilitates bonding among children, teacher, and parents."[66]

Focused and regular professional development for teachers is also a component of Woodland's instructional program. Once a month, the school closes

---

66. Woodland Elementary Charter School, Renewal application, 2006: 74.

early and teachers participate in professional development. Professional development reportedly "improves student achievement by allowing more time for professional learning communities, vertical teaming, staff training, team planning, and parent conferences."[67]

Individuals interviewed attribute the school's success with children with disabilities to the integration of (1) TAG instructional techniques, (2) a commitment to teacher accountability based on a data-driven culture, (3) ongoing training and collaboration between general education and special education, and (4) an explicit expectation that all parents volunteer at the school.

CONCLUSION

All six of these schools have distinct purposes, student populations, and contexts. We chose them in part to illustrate how differently students with disabilities can be served, even within the charter school sector. On the other hand, there are also important similarities in how these schools approach special education. The next chapter provides an analysis of the common approaches and explores the question, "Could traditional public schools and school districts adopt similar practices?"

---

67. Ibid.

Chapter 5

Lessons from Successful Charter Schools

Lauren Morando Rhim and Dana Brinson

Despite their very different approaches, the six schools described in chapter 4 have much in common in the way they serve students with disabilities and what makes it possible for teachers to be successful with diverse student needs.[68] Surprisingly, though, we saw that many of the common attributes of these schools extended well beyond practices thought to be effective in special education and could easily be thought of as best practices for meeting the needs of all students. These broad characteristics included:

- schoolwide commitment to serving special needs,
- effective professional supports for teachers,
- customized student interventions and services,
- a focus on effective instructional strategies over individualized education program (IEP) status, and
- safe and respectful student-to-student interactions.

These attributes are common to any kind of successful school but may be even more important for ensuring that schools serve their students with disabilities well. Other promising characteristics in the schools we visited were unique to the needs of students eligible for special education. For example, several programs we encountered distinguished themselves by creating an effective inclusionary environment and supports for students with disabilities.

The fact that charter schools are usually started from scratch, are small, and can select their own teaching staff is likely an advantage for creating and sustaining innovative practices. It is also clear, however, that traditional public schools should pay close attention to these strategies and not consider them simply a function of the charter environment. In fact, there was a resounding affirmation among the teachers and school leaders we interviewed that these programs could be successfully implemented in district schools *as long as* they were accompanied by the support of the district and ongoing commitment to appropriate professional development and training necessary to effectively run

---

68. Our selection methodology is described in chapter 4.

the programs. Of particular note, because the strategies used in these schools were usually geared toward all students served in the schools, not just those with formal IEPs, an important result may be improved learning outcomes not only for students with disabilities but for struggling, average, and gifted students as well.

The following sections explore these themes and present specific evidence from the individual case study schools.

COMMON ATTRIBUTES OF SUCCESSFUL SPECIAL EDUCATION IN CHARTER SCHOOLS

Schoolwide Commitment to Meet Individual Needs

Charter schools are different from traditional public schools in that founders must propose to run a school with a specific purpose, be it to prepare their students for college or to become independent thinkers. This mission-driven nature can help teachers by replacing an environment focused on old habits and assumptions with one that places mission above all else. Across the six schools, we observed school missions and culture that fostered (1) leadership's commitment to a philosophy of inclusion, (2) a sense of ownership for all students, and (3) a commitment to complying with the spirit of the Individuals with Disabilities Education Act (IDEA) of 2004 as a starting point rather than a postscript.

Leadership's Commitment to Inclusion
School leaders at five of the six case study schools expressed a core commitment to incorporating children with disabilities in the overall school program, whether or not the schools were originally designed with a special education focus.

Several schools—CHIME Arnold Schwarzenegger Charter Elementary and Middle Schools, Metro Deaf School (MDS), and Charyl Stockwell Academy (CSA)—were designed with special education populations foremost in the thinking of their founders. Not surprisingly, leaders at all of these schools had developed an infrastucture and set of processes to maximize student opportunity and potential within the school. CSA, for example, provides comprehensive evaluation and early interventions that, in many cases, have reduced or removed the need for special education services and labeling.

The two CHIME schools grew out of a pilot program developed at California State University, Northridge, explicitly designed to develop inclusive instructional environments supported by co-teaching. CHIME's core commitment to inclusion is part of its mission and reflected in every aspect of its program (e.g., teacher and parent handbook, marketing materials, hiring process, and professional development). In addition, CHIME strives to serve as a model that other schools can emulate and incorporates research and teaching others about their model into the program. The schools are a training site for student teachers and the school has produced a DVD about developing IEPs for inclusive settings.

In the three case study schools for which special education was not a key factor in program design (Roxbury Preparatory, ISUS Institute of Construction Technology, and Woodland Elementary), children with disabilities appeared to succeed because school leaders are committed to full inclusion and ensuring that the general education programs work for all students.

Roxbury Preparatory and ISUS provide small classrooms, individualized education, and integrated behavioral programs that stress self-control and mutual respect. Woodland's extensive use of Talented-and-Gifted (TAG) teaching strategies and high degree of teacher accountability were credited with boosting academic performance for all students. The school leaders, teachers, and parents we spoke with at these schools believed that these factors created an environment where students with disabilities can be as successful as their typically developing peers.

Widespread Teacher Commitment to Inclusion
Traditionally, general education teachers have not considered it their responsibility to teach students with special needs, instead referring these students to specific programs or teachers in the school who provided extra supports or interventions. In contrast, teachers at four of the schools in our study expressed a striking sense of ownership and responsibility for the achievement of students with disabilities. They felt responsible for the education of *all* of their students and did not abdicate their responsibility for a specific student simply because a special educator was in the classroom to provide assistance to the child. At CHIME, for example, parents reported that under the co-teaching model, their child did not differentiate at all between the general and special education teacher. During observations of CHIME classrooms, we could not determine which teacher was the general versus special educator because they appeared to share responsibility for the group as a whole *as well as* individualized instruction in the classroom.

At Charyl Stockwell Academy, teachers have open and ongoing relationships with parents and the Teacher Support Team to facilitate conversations about student needs. Parents of twins who had been identified with autism when they were two commented that their children's general education teacher would call them up and say, "Something happened today and I was hoping you could help me figure out how to approach the situation if it happens again." This close working relationship is a cornerstone of the support services at CSA. The parents reported that both of their children, now age nine, have a strong social network, are reading at or near high-school level and no longer require special education.

At Roxbury Prep, building a sense of ownership among teachers for the academic success of all students begins with rigorous hiring practices that identify teachers who are committed to the program's full-inclusion policy. Because all students with disabilities are in the general education classroom nearly 100 percent of the time, the co-director explained, it is critical that teachers understand from the start that the education of students with disabilities is primarily their responsibility.

Commitment to Tenets of IDEA

Rather than viewing IDEA as a law for which they had to demonstrate procedural compliance alone, personnel at the schools we studied saw the law as a starting point. The spirit of the law—to provide students with disabilities equal access to education alongside their peers without disabilities—was the focus, rather than merely meeting the letter of the law.

At Roxbury Prep, for example, "college for certain" is the goal for all Roxbury Prep students, and through the individualized approach each student—regardless of ability or disability—is given the remediation, instruction, and supplemental activities he or she needs to develop college-ready skills. All student-level progress data are closely monitored by the faculty and administration and used to guide the curriculum as well as individualized evaluation and instruction.

In the case of Metro Deaf School, where all the students are deaf or hard of hearing, it may seem at first that the school does not adhere to an inclusive view of special education or the tenets of a "least restrictive environment." The founders and leaders at Metro Deaf, however, believe that providing students with hearing impairments an environment in which they can communicate with every student and staff member via American Sign Language (ASL) *is* providing the least restrictive environment in which their students can learn. They believe that access to fluent ASL communicators develops the students' abilities to express themselves, progress academically, and develop the social skills necessary to succeed in the world.

The founder of Charyl Stockwell Academy admitted he was not always a supporter of strict compliance with the procedural aspects of special education law; he felt that compliance could be met and students' needs still ignored. To address the gap between compliance and education, he sought to develop a school that did provide the least restrictive, fully inclusive, and highly individualized academic environment that was necessary for every student to learn at his or her greatest potential. In this sense, the school reflects a true commitment to what we consider the core intent of IDEA and *No Child Left Behind.*

Strong Support for Teachers

The attributes described above are simple enough in concept but may be nearly impossible to implement without help for teachers to (1) understand their responsibilities toward students with disabilities and (2) evaluate their own impact on student learning for all students. Building on the overall commitment to students with disabilities and the core tenets of IDEA, school leaders in our case studies reported focusing on specialized professional development and data-driven decisionmaking.

Targeted and Relevant Professional Development

Leaders and special educators at all of the case study schools identified targeted, relevant professional development as key to implementing a successful special education program and as an important element of building buy-in from all teachers related to educating children with disabilities. Two weeks of professional development at the beginning of the year and half-day professional development and teacher collaboration every week at Charyl Stockwell Academy provided teachers ample opportunities to learn not only about effective implementation of the school's Teacher Support Team program but also about indicators of learning problems, specific disabilities, and appropriate interventions.

Routine professional development is also a hallmark of Roxbury Prep's program where the special education coordinator noted that requests from general education teachers guide their professional development sessions. For example, the special education coordinator provided training on non-verbal learning disabilities at the request of the teaching staff.

Metro Deaf School requires an intensive ASL teaching methods program for new teachers to promote effective ASL fluency in their students. In addition, MDS's special education teacher provides information, training, and guidance to teachers who have students with dual/multiple disabilities in their classroom.

The special education director at ISUS Institute of Construction Technology strives to build the general educators' confidence in the referral process and make certain that the teachers recognize that they cannot use special education referrals to shift responsibility for a student to the special education staff members.

Data-Based Decisionmaking

Every case study school reported using formative assessment or other diagnostic data to inform and influence instruction and interventions. For three schools, ongoing assessment and analysis played a central role in their intervention strategies.

At Charyl Stockwell Academy, pre- and post-intervention testing enables school personnel to evaluate the efficacy of interventions. The data inform not only the services given to the child, but are also collected in aggregate to identify those resources that work most effectively with their students. A secure web-based database houses individual student assessment data that are retrieved when the Teacher Support Team discusses individual students. The database provides an at-a-glance view of every assessment conducted, with scores, as well as each intervention implemented and the results.

Woodland Elementary personnel we spoke to viewed data as central to their classroom decisionmaking and critical to holding teachers accountable for their instructional practices. Special education administrator Jackie Radford explained that, "Our curriculum specialist receives [test] scores and makes comments back to the teachers. She makes recommendations about instruction . . . . Sometimes it might require additional staff development so she might suggest a course. We use test scores to change instruction. We are very data-driven. It is crucial to our success."

Customized Student Services

Five of the six case study schools provide highly individualized programs for *all* of their students, general and special education alike. This individualization essentially takes the stigma out of being part of special education because all students receive individualized services, not just those with an IEP. This "normalization" of individualized education also appeared to facilitate access to the general education curriculum and academic success for students with disabilities by encouraging teachers to accommodate a variety of learning needs.

At CHIME charter schools, there is little to no demarcation between general and special education. All children are provided with an individual learning plan (an IEP—individualized *education* program—for children with disabilities and an individualized *instructional* program for children without disabilities). Each classroom has general and special education teaching teams. Parents of CHIME students remarked that the school removes labels and their children refer to their friends by a variety of traits (e.g., brown hair, freckles, or tall) but never by their disability. The parents viewed this lack of labeling as an indication that children with disabilities are seamlessly included at the school.

At Roxbury Prep, all students are tutored and individually mentored, a process that mirrors the individual supports provided to students in special education. For this reason, co-director Dana Lehman noted, most students at Roxbury Prep do not know who is and who is not identified for special education services. Individualized services follow Roxbury Prep students even after they graduate the 8th grade. The Graduate Services Program (GSP) works with its former students as they navigate the college selection and application process and serves as a support system while those students are in college. Roxbury Prep's leaders believe that this intensive, long-term assistance has significantly contributed to the fact that all of their graduates who had been identified for special education services graduated high school and enrolled in college.

At Charyl Stockwell Academy, it is not unusual for students working next to each other to be completing different assignments; students with disabilities are not singled out. Principal Shelley Stockwell noted that this is how CSA can seamlessly incorporate special education services into what is "normal" at the school, thereby further decreasing any potential stigmatization that may accompany the label of "special education."

Focus on Effective, Not Segmented, Instructional Practices

Just as they applied the concept of individualized instructional plans to all students, our case study schools also found that best instructional practices for children *without* disabilities benefit children *with* disabilities and vice versa. Personnel from several case study schools found that interventions typically noted in IEPs (e.g., written directions, assistance with organizational skills, behavioral modification, and redirection) can benefit students without disabilities and, when implemented in the general education classroom, can facilitate a full-inclusion program.

At Roxbury Prep, the co-director noted that special education works at Roxbury Prep because general education works at Roxbury Prep. The plan for each class and homework assignments are written on the blackboard, students are assisted with keeping a school planner, and everyone is reminded to read through the directions. In addition, the school's strict behavioral program provides redirection to all students, not just those with an IEP. Such supports, school personnel reported, benefit all students and the orderly environment can promote inclusion of students with disabilities for whom these supports are necessary and outlined in an IEP.

At Woodland Elementary, school leadership has explicitly and nearly universally incorporated TAG teaching approaches throughout the school. Instructional approaches designed for gifted students provide new and varied strategies for teaching academic content. The TAG coordinator reflected, "It is very rewarding to hear from a teacher that special education and ESL kids are excelling with the TAG. They will come up with the response. Wow, [without the TAG training] the teacher may have missed out on that kind of teaching for a child."

Safe and Respectful Environment

Ultimately, individualized programs, intensive teacher training, and the normalization of individual help would be meaningless in an environment that did not feel safe and inclusive for students with special needs. A purposeful culture of respect was considered central at five of the six case study schools. These schools cultivated the feeling of "family" in addition to no-tolerance policies on teasing, bullying, and disrespectful behavior—attributes likely fostered by the relatively small size of the five schools. Individuals who identified a safe environment as a central part of their school's success argued that if students are afraid to try, they will never have the opportunity to succeed.

At ISUS, morning and afternoon "family meetings" allow students to share concerns, publicly thank people, or call out those who have been disrespectful. School personnel reported that this daily routine helps students learn to effectively deal with conflict and come to understand that their behavior has consequences. They believe these meetings—in addition to therapy, training and support in developing self-control, and life skills courses—combine to foster an atmosphere of mutual respect among the students and with the staff. Ann Higdon proudly noted, "Even though 80 percent of our students have been court involved, there are no metal detectors in this school. Students know they are safe here and that they do not have to bring weapons to protect themselves."

Roxbury Prep has a no-tolerance policy for teasing or laughing at others, using derogatory terms like "retarded" or "sped," or play-fighting. Students who break these rules, even once, are suspended. Co-director Dana Lehman explained that because they make a big deal out of little things, they do not have to deal with bigger issues. The special education teachers reflected that no-tolerance policies have created an atmosphere where students with disabilities feel safe. One noted that even her students who read excruciatingly slowly are proud to read aloud and are comfortable doing so because they know they will be treated with respect and kindness.

Even at Metro Deaf School, where 100 percent of the students have a disability, tolerance training is necessary to promote a supportive and inclusive environment. For instance, special education coordinator Kelly Anderson simulated for the students what it would be like to be deaf and also have autism or be legally blind. For the autism simulation, Anderson had the students sit on four tennis balls (to make them feel unbalanced), pinned itchy material in the backs of their shirts (like a clothing tag), flashed the lights on and off rapidly, and signed "at the speed of light" on an unfamiliar topic. Students who participated in this demonstration later reported feelings of empathy for their peers with autism, stating, "it must be really hard to learn with those distractions." MDS teachers saw students demonstrate greater patience with peers with multiple disabilities after that experience.

TRANSFERABILITY TO TRADITIONAL PUBLIC SCHOOLS

While in some cases the schools' status as charter schools may have facilitated ready adoption of promising practices, there is no apparent reason why traditional public schools could not adopt very similar approaches. In fact, personnel at all six schools proposed that their programs could be replicated in traditional public schools as long as such schools are deeply committed to change and have (1) the ability to build their own teaching team, (2) adequate resources, and (3) strategies to involve parents.

Ability to Craft a Team

Four of the six school leaders we spoke with noted that autonomy from district policies and procedures and, specifically, collective bargaining agreements (the ability to hire and/or fire teachers) can be an extremely valuable asset to developing a cohesive team of teachers committed to the school's general and special education programs. Yet, personnel from two of the schools that operated within the parameter of district personnel policies (CHIME and Woodland Elementary), noted that they were able to successfully hire and train instructional personnel to support their school mission even absent broad autonomy—a skill arguably utilized by most strong school leaders.

At CHIME, potential applicants need to be willing to share a classroom with their co-teaching counterpart—not always a natural situation for all teachers. Furthermore, they have to buy into the full-inclusion model and be flexible enough to manage potentially multiple paraeducators and student teachers in their classroom. While not a prerequisite for employment, the majority of the teachers at CHIME had been trained in, or had experience with, co-teaching.

Co-director Lehman at Roxbury Prep noted that she had 200 applications for four teacher slots one year. Despite the number of applicants, she said it was difficult to find teachers who would fit in with the disciplined approach of the school and who could commit the time and effort necessary to bring 6th graders from behind and make them ready for a college preparatory high school by 8th grade.

In addition to control over hiring, the ability to fire or not renew teachers is another benefit of freedom from collective bargaining agreements that case study principals appreciated. Director Stockwell of Charyl Stockwell Academy noted that she does not renew on average one teacher per year. She stressed, however, that it is not necessarily because the person is a poor teacher, but because the teacher is a poor fit for their specific program and approach.

Appropriate Resources to Train and Support Teachers

Aside from an initial investment in professional development, three of the six schools we studied (CSA, Roxbury Prep, and Woodland) pay for their special education programs with the same or fewer revenues than other public schools receive. The other three schools, which primarily serve students with disabilities or specific challenges (CHIME, ISUS, and MDS), require additional resources to support their instructional model.

To manage costs, Charyl Stockwell Academy tries to minimize the number of students identified as needing formal special education services by focusing on early intervention and preventive services. One of the founders of CSA noted that if districts could decrease the number of students who require special education services by providing timely, short-term, and intensive interventions, districts could potentially save millions of dollars and provide better services and educational opportunities to their students. About 8 percent of the students at CSA are identified for special education; this is in stark contrast to the state average of about 14.4 percent and the regional average of nearly 16 percent.

At Woodland, arguably the most traditional of the six case study schools, staff had used the autonomy granted by their charter to alter their existing budget to support TAG training for all teachers. While the school initially enjoyed a transfusion of dollars from the federal charter school program when it first converted to charter status, the school no longer qualifies for these dollars.

As for the more specialized and more expensive programs, additional costs for low class sizes and specialized supports were paid for through state or local special education allocations (because the majority or all students qualify for special education), as well as external donors and in-kind donations.

The cost of ISUS, for example, was $17,000 per student, paid for by the state, plus an annual donor- and grant-funded budget of $800,000 for community construction projects. The total cost of educating an ISUS student was nearly triple the average cost per student in the district. However, the program provides a unique vocational training program in which ISUS students can learn every aspect of working in the construction industry and contribute new housing and other assets to the community. ISUS founder Ann Higdon argued that the short- and long-term results with ISUS students are well worth the initial investment.

Strategies for Engaging Parents

A recurring assumption about charter schools is that high levels of parental involvement typically associated with schools of choice are integral to their success. This was not the case for the schools we studied. The six case study schools encourage parental involvement, as most schools do, but they do not appear to rely heavily on parental involvement for their schools' successes.

At Metro Deaf School, some students commute from an hour away to attend the school and their parents may not use American Sign Language or even speak English. MDS was focused on reaching out more to parents, but recognized that, like most schools, it has a blend of parental involvement, from highly to rarely involved, and their program must continue to thrive for the students regardless of the levels of parental support.

At ISUS, a drop-out recovery program, parents may not even be present in their children's lives. ISUS actively nurtures a close-knit atmosphere at the school to compensate for this frequent lack of family support. Twice-daily "family meetings," student self and peer redirection, and life-skills coaching work together to make the students what Ann Higdon calls "transcenders." Through these types of in-school supports, she noted, students develop the skills necessary to transcend their limitations—academic, social, and familial—and learn to become self-reliant.

Ironically, Woodland Elementary—the one charter school in our study that was formerly a traditional public school, and the school we found to be most similar to large traditional public elementary schools—relied the most notably on parental involvement and required that all parents contribute 10 volunteer hours each year. However, the parental role was valued generally as opposed to specifically for students with disabilities. The school employs a parental involvement coordinator and the volunteers' hours are monitored electronically. Parents are offered multiple different opportunities (both in school and outside of school) to meet the volunteer hour commitment and parents are credited with supporting the school's success.

Opportunities for Replicating Practices in District or Other Charter Schools

All school personnel we interviewed were optimistic that the innovative or best practices documented in the case study schools could be adopted in traditional or other charter public schools *if* leadership is committed to developing strong special education programs. Below we briefly highlight the approaches we saw that are most adaptable to another school as well as potential barriers to transferability.

At Charyl Stockwell Academy, school leaders had already begun to disseminate the Teacher Support Team program and were working on disseminating their Smart Character Choices program. They have found that their Teacher Support Team program can accommodate different theories, approaches, and interventions while the core approaches—early assessment, intensive and short-term interventions, and reassessment—can be applied anywhere, but will likely require intensive initial staff development.

The CHIME model of full inclusion could, according to staff there, be adopted in other schools if leadership is genuinely committed to the idea that *all* children can benefit from rigorous individualized instruction in inclusive classrooms. However, districts may also need to replicate the schools' partnership with a local university to assure a strong supply of qualified personnel to support the intensive inclusion model.

Personnel from Metro Deaf School contended that their dual-language approach could easily be transferred to self-contained deaf education classrooms in districts provided there was a "critical mass" of students to facilitate language acquisition. To replicate MDS, another school would also have to resist the more typical fractured approach to deaf education practiced in public schools and limit themselves to one proven method alone—the dual-language approach—and not employ other approaches or tools for deaf education.

Personnel in all of the other schools we studied similarly asserted that their models could easily be adopted in other public schools.

CONCLUSION

Our research inquiry was based on the hypothesis that charter schools can use their autonomy to develop and implement innovative and effective practices for children with disabilities. While not all of the practices are innovative, they do appear to reflect established best practices (e.g., early intervention strategies, supportive school culture, and co-teaching) that can be observed in other good schools, traditional and charter alike. While some of the schools have intentionally created successful programs for children with disabilities, other schools have simply created schoolwide programs designed to benefit children with and without disabilities.

The schools appeared to be leveraging their charter autonomy to select their own teaching staffs and maintain a small school size to implement a clear, unifying focus and school culture to serve their students' needs. These schools also benefited from the ability to do things (e.g., raise money for the construction program and control the allocation of funds within their building) without having to overcome the bureaucratic hurdles traditional public school administrators would have to overcome to introduce similar changes.

In theory, administrators could restructure traditional public schools to do these things, but union contracts, centralized budgeting, and bureaucracy may be significant barriers. They would also require significant commitment on the part of school and district leaders to overcome any resistance from general educators and to build their skill sets.

Interestingly, the cases also reflected the diversity of philosophies and convictions related to special education. For instance, CHIME is based on a commitment to inclusive classrooms for all students with disabilities while at the other end of the spectrum, Metro Deaf School is based on an explicit separation of children who are deaf or hearing impaired from children without hearing impairments. In contrast, Woodland operates a relatively traditional special education program with both inclusive and self-contained classrooms and Charyl Stockwell explicitly strives to decrease the number of students identified to receive special education services. Yet, all the programs appear to have demonstrated a degree of success with their student population that is noteworthy.

We are limited in our ability to generalize about these exploratory case studies, but we think it is significant to acknowledge the fundamental diversity of the approaches these schools employ and the success they enjoy educating students with disabilities. These approaches can be successful in educating children with disabilities and, more broadly, educating all children.

Additional in-depth research is required to track the academic progress of children with disabilities in charter schools and thereafter, and investigate instructional and organizational practices that correlate with exemplary academic outcomes.

Chapter 6

A Challenge for Charters: Meeting Student Needs and Parent Expectations

LAUREN MORANDO RHIM

Despite striking success stories such as those discussed in the previous chapter, charter schools encounter many of the same challenges in offering special education as traditional public schools.[69] For example, charter schools struggle to hire and retain qualified special education and related services personnel, to understand the plethora of procedural requirements, and to develop high-quality programs with limited resources.

Due to their charter status, these schools also face additional issues associated with their unique status as generally small, independent, mission-driven schools of choice. Broadly, yet succinctly, Carolyn Sullins and Gary Miron characterize charter schools' dilemma related to special education this way: "How can charter schools be equitable to students with all types of needs, while remaining financially viable and true to their educational mission?"[70]

The emerging literature and interviews with key informants identify both procedural and operational challenges that undermine the ability of charter schools to serve as viable options for children with disabilities.

PROCEDURAL CHALLENGES

Special education is defined by procedures dictated by multiple laws, regulations, and standard operating practices. These procedures pose notable challenges for charter school operators who may be unfamiliar with public school administration. The procedural challenges fall into two categories: lack of clarity about legal responsibility and limited access to standard service infrastructures.

---

69. See for example: Ahearn et al., 2001; Downing, Spencer, and Cavallaire, 2004; Finn, Manno, and Vanourek, 2000; McLaughlin and Henderson, 1998; Miron and Nelson, 2002; Rhim, Lange, Ahearn, and McLaughlin, 2007a; Rhim, Lange, Ahearn, and McLaughlin, 2007b.

70. Sullins and Miron, 2005, 113.

Lack of Clarity

Legal responsibility for educating children with disabilities is derived from an amalgam of federal, state, and district policies and practices. Due to the multiple sources of policies and practices, there is variability in interpretation and implementation of the laws across, and even within, states. Elizabeth Giovannetti, a clinical social worker with Educational Support Systems and consultant to charter schools explained:

> It is not just IDEA [Individuals with Disabilities Education Act (IDEA) of 2004], you have the state and local regulations, and the LEA [local education agency] and non-LEA issue. There are responsibilities under each of these umbrellas. Understanding policy issues, helping schools understand all the relationships and what are they left with in terms of responsibility is critical. You have to get everyone to understand how that works, and in every unique situation. Schools need to understand these relationships as they build their program.

Nelson Smith of the National Alliance for Public Charter Schools also identified lack of knowledge of special education law as a key impediment and noted, "Mastering the education law is hard even for districts with lots of resources."

Confounding the variability are inherent tensions in the charter sector associated with the heavily regulated nature of special education and the goal of deregulation that is central to the charter school concept.[71] That is, not all charter operators understand their responsibilities associated with IDEA, specifically, the heavy reliance on process and inputs rather than outputs. For example, IDEA dictates very specific timelines and procedures that schools must abide by when referring a child for special education and subsequently, developing an individualized education program (IEP) for the child (i.e., the inputs). In turn, special education monitoring tracks the degree to which schools abide by the timelines and procedures with arguably minimal attention to the academic outcomes (i.e., outputs). Multiple informants acknowledged that contributing to this lack of understanding is a less than universal commitment to educating children with disabilities. However, this is not unique to the charter sector.[72]

Anecdotal evidence from the field indicates that charter school operators have gained a better understanding of their responsibilities over time (see sidebar). State departments of education and charter authorizers have played a key role in raising charter applicants' awareness of their responsibilities related to children with disabilities and communicating the importance of incorporating special education in

---

71. Heubert, 1997, 301–53; Ahearn et al., 2001.

72. For a discussion of the conceptualization of disability and varying levels of commitment to the notion that all children can learn, see: Andrews et al., 2000, 258–60, 267; and National Council on Disability, 2008.

their charter development plans. Nevertheless, in some states, charter schools must also contend with hostility on the part of traditional districts that are opposed to the creation of charter schools and may not take proactive steps that could help them succeed. Dan Quisenberry of the Michigan Charter Schools Association noted, "We have a traditional education system that does not know how to respond. How do we respond to these schools? What are schools responsible for doing? How do we allow schools to be creative and access services?"

Authorizers, particularly inexperienced authorizers, sometimes compound the lack of clarity. Smith noted:

Authorizers have to be a lot clearer about the responsibilities of charter schools. They have to write the legal responsibilities directly into their charters and it has to be written in the contract. The authorizer who writes a charter has to clarify who will hold [schools] responsible for what. When you have a school board that authorizes, they may put language about [special education] in a charter pro forma, but the execution falls to the school district and the school district treats the charter school as a step-child so execution is weak. With non-district authorizers, they often have to learn themselves, so they may try to be clearer about what the execution should look like as well.

Susie Miller Barker of the National Association of Charter School Authorizers commented:

Where you have alternative authorizers who are not familiar with special education, they don't have the systems to provide education services. Problems can arise when identifying a child, and constructing the local

"In some ways, the field has evolved. When things first started, there was a battle about whether special education has to occur in charter schools. This is gone. I don't hear those comments as much as I did years ago. Initially, people were pretty unabashed about saying that charter schools don't have to offer special education. The congressional action in 1999 [IDEA regulations], made it crystal clear. From a federal definition, if you want federal funding, you have to provide special education. This real and symbolic message is influential. [Nevertheless], there is still quite a bit of uncertainty about how it applies. We are making gains in terms of considering special education as a design feature. We still run into applicants who have not thought about special education within the innovative charter school idea. I think this is getting better. States are getting better."—*Julie Mead, University of Wisconsin*

special education team . . . . It is much more direct when it is an SEA [State Education Agency] or LEA authorizer. These folks know about special education. In a place where there are special-purpose or university authorizers, the capacity is not as immediate.

There are also questions surrounding the legal identity of charter schools and the responsibility associated with this identity. If the state charter school law is unambiguous and charter schools are independent LEAs, legal responsibility may be relatively clear. However, all of the informants interviewed noted that, when a charter school is part of an existing school district, there are at best questions and at worst contentious debates about who is responsible for what.

Clarity about funding special education for charter schools is another challenge. For instance, in Maryland, local districts authorize charter schools and retain ultimate responsibility for ensuring compliance with IDEA. The state charter school law requires that districts provide charter schools with "commensurate funding," including special education dollars. But what does "commensurate" mean? Does the term apply to services or to funds? Contending that "commensurate" did not mean services (over which charter schools could exercise little control) but actual dollars, charter operators initiated litigation against their authorizing district to seek clarity about the definition.

In 2006, the courts ruled that "commensurate" includes funds generally allocated for a variety of central office services and entails actual dollars rather than services in lieu of dollars.[73] In practical terms, charter schools in Baltimore were initially allocated $5,011 in cash and $2,943 in services per pupil, but after the ruling, an appeal, and a final decision by the Court of Appeals, the per-pupil allocation increased to $10,956.[74] The conflict demonstrates a challenge charter schools face when school districts interpret state charter school statutes in a manner that can limit the school's ability to fulfill its full mission.

Understanding charter schools' responsibilities under IDEA requires an operational understanding of IDEA and related state special education and charter school laws.[75] Absent explicit discussions with—and guidance provided by—authorizers before, during, and after the charter application process, charter school operators are struggling to decipher the extent of their legal responsibilities and thereafter implement policies that comply with the law. As Barry Barnett of the Massachusetts Department of Education put it, the key issue is: "Where is the line between charter and district responsibilities?"

Evidence from the charter sector reveals several severe consequences of this lack of clarity. First, it may lead to charter students with disabilities not

---

73. *Baltimore City Board of School Commissioners v. City Neighbors Charter School.* 2006.

74. Tamber, 2007.

75. Green and Mead, 2004.

receiving services they need. Giovannetti noted that due to the highly litigious nature of special education and the laws that govern service delivery, new charter operators are often "afraid of what they don't know about special education." Rather than drilling down to identify instructional solutions to meet students' unique learning requirements, decisions may be influenced by fear. Giovannetti explained that "the fear of special education keeps new school leaders from believing that they can create an environment in which all students can learn—but they can. And if they do that, there is nothing to fear."

Fear on the part of charter operators can also lead to "counseling out" children with disabilities, advising parents that they cannot or should not enroll their child in a particular school. Allegations of counseling out have been an area of concern since the early days of the charter movement.[76] National survey data indicates that 3 percent of charter schools have openly told parents that they cannot enroll their child because of their disability and 44 percent admitted to advising parents that another school might offer more appropriate services.[77] This is a situation rife with the possibility of creating problems for charter schools. More than that, unwillingness to serve children with disabilities is illegal and harmful to children.

High-stakes accountability measures that hold schools accountable for subgroups of students who have been marginalized in the past add to the problem. *No Child Left Behind* (NCLB) shines a bright light on programs such as special education, and ideally pushes all schools to internalize a commitment to all students. Yet, for all of its laudable goals, the legislation's high-stakes measures can have the unintended consequence of serving as a disincentive to enroll children with disabilities, especially if charter operators lack confidence that they can meet their needs. This disincentive may be particularly potent in charter schools due to the added accountability built into renewable charter contracts and fear of not making "adequate yearly progress" with the potential penalty of losing the charter.

Overcoming the fear of failure in special education is a significant challenge for charter schools. Paul O'Neill of Edison Schools summarized the angst of many charter school operators around the issue:

> *There is a lack of clarity about what is required to serve students with disabilities in charter schools.... Charter schools are worried. It is expensive and difficult to orchestrate. There is a danger of counseling out. You never quite know ... do I have to create a special class? Do I have to take all kids? And, by the way, it all costs money. Charter schools don't know.*

---

76. Ahearn et al., 2001; Fiore et al., 2000; McKinney, 1996, 22–25; McLaughlin and Henderson, 1998, 99–107; Miron and Nelson, 2002; Wells et al., 1998.
77. Rhim, Lange, Ahearn, and McLaughlin, 2007a.

They are trying to fulfill a mission with the school and they say, 'We can't serve that kid and create this mission with the law and the goodwill of the community and parents.'

While struggling to understand legal responsibilities associated with special education is not necessarily unique to the charter sector, informants reported that they see this challenge as *more prominent* in charter schools due to the newness of the sector, the mission-driven nature of charter schools, and the lack experience of many charter school leaders.

Limited Access to Support Structures

State education systems are comprised of multiple levels of systems and supports that have evolved over time to support districts and schools. These include intermediate agencies, such as intermediate school districts in Michigan or boards of cooperative education services in Colorado and New York. These publicly funded entities are typically charged with providing a host of services to multiple districts, including special education.

Due to the fact that statutory language pertaining to the intermediate agencies was drafted prior to development of charter schools or due to resistance on the part of personnel in these agencies, charter schools are not able to fully access these intermediate agencies in many states. The lack of access may impact multiple areas of charter school operations but the impact on special education programs is particularly notable given the complexity and costs associated with developing programs. Our research revealed multiple examples of barriers due to (1) charter schools not being afforded the same access to state special education service support systems that state law and regulations require and (2) intermediate districts limiting charter schools' access to resources and services. State-specific examples illustrate the challenges that arise due to these barriers.

Legal and Regulatory Hurdles

The literature and interviews revealed multiple examples of charter schools having inadequate access to state service and support structures due to statutory limitations. For instance, special education cooperatives are a popular strategy in many states (e.g., California, Colorado, Illinois, Kansas, Massachusetts, Minnesota, and New York). These cooperatives, also referred to as collaboratives, permit school districts to pool their resources, distribute risk, and maximize special education expertise and resources. While the specifics vary by state and even individual cooperative, in general, members join voluntarily and pay an annual fee to access the services the cooperative provides. In some states, districts provide most special education services themselves but rely on cooperatives for technical assistance and professional development, as well as related services personnel and services for children with low-incidence disabilities.

In Massachusetts, special education cooperatives predate the state charter law, which was passed in 1993. These collaboratives pool resources to buy a lot of things: direct services to students, management support, cooperative purchasing, transportation, research, technology development, the implementation of health and safety programs, and professional development.[78]

Since state policy guidance on collaboratives predates the establishment of charter schools, the state does not list charter schools as one of the entities permitted to form or join a special education collaborative. Although the law and state guidance is silent on the matter, the omission is interpreted to mean that charter schools are not allowed to form or join collaboratives. So, charter schools are not permitted to take advantage of a key mechanism traditional public schools use to extend their financial and technical expertise for children with disabilities.

Barnett of the Massachusetts Department of Education described the consequence of the exclusion: "Charter schools [are] forbidden from forming collaboratives . . . [C]harter schools are on the outside looking in. They cannot join a co-op, cannot form a collaborative, and cannot share costs. The policy solution is to change the co-op law." Until the legal and regulatory structure is changed, charter school costs may be higher and their services to students with disabilities may be limited.

The situation in New York's Boards of Cooperative Educational Services (BOCES) is very similar. According to Jennifer Sneed of the State University of New York's (SUNY's) Charter Schools Institute: "BOCES have a myriad of programs and staff for special education . . . occupational therapy, lots of services and programs, but the state law does not allow charter schools to access the services. [Charter schools] are excluded from the services of this intermediate education agency." As a result of the exclusion, if the child has an IEP and requires services that a district would typically obtain from their BOCES, the charter school would have to purchase the services at market rate outside of the public system—or the student would have to leave the charter school in order to obtain those services through the district. In June of 2007, the State Education Department recommended that the state statute be amended to give BOCES the authority to provide charter schools with the same services, at cost, that public school districts receive.[79]

---

78. Commonwealth of Massachusetts, General Laws of Massachusetts, 2006.

79. Duncan-Poitier, J. 2007, 52.

Service Agencies Limit Access to Resources

Statutes and regulations are not the only problem. We came across multiple examples of resistance to charters schools on the part of the traditional public school systems and the intermediate service agencies developed to support them.

In California, state and federal special education funds are directed to local school districts via a system of Special Education Local Plan Areas (SELPAS). All school districts are required to belong to a SELPA and charter schools that wish to operate as independent districts must first apply to a SELPA, which is permitted to reject applications for membership.

The regulations governing SELPAS were developed prior to the introduction of charter schools; consequently, the regulations do not anticipate creation of multiple new school districts or non-geographically proximate member districts. Amendments to state statute since the introduction of charter schools affirm that when considering applications for membership from charter schools, SELPAS "may not treat the charter school differently from the manner in which it treats a similar request made by a district school."[80] While some SELPAS have been willing to accept charter schools as members, many have not.

According to Eileen Ahearn of the National Association of State Directors of Special Education, charter advocates and the California Department of Education are in the process of creating an all-charter-school SELPA or a traditional SELPA that serves multiple charter schools across the state.

In Michigan, charter schools reportedly have intermittent access to regional service providers due to lack of understanding about charter schools and their instructional approaches and resistance on the part of some intermediate units to working with charter schools. Intermediate school districts (ISDs) in Michigan are required to provide schools in their geographic catchment area with special education programs, professional development, and technical assistance. However, as Teri Pettit of the Michigan Association of Public School Academies explained, "Some ISDs were providing ancillary services [e.g., speech and occupational therapy] to all schools in the district but denying it to their charter schools." Our interviews revealed that tensions between ISDs and charter schools can develop:

- if charter schools attempt to approach special education differently;
- when disagreements about allocation of funds for special education develop, especially around whether ISDs retain funds and provide services or forward the funds to the schools;
- where charter schools seek Medicaid reimbursement for special education services, which the ISD refuses to approve; or

---

80. California Education Code, Section §47645.

- when ISD resistance to working with charter schools causes bottlenecks and denies schools and students access to resources and services.

These challenges are more than mere irritants; they can also have tangible negative effects on charter school operations. Lack of access to intermediate units may preclude charter schools from becoming independent, increase costs of special education services, decrease access to professional development and technical assistance, and deny services to children who need them.

OPERATIONAL CHALLENGES

Operational challenges are at least as difficult as procedural roadblocks. Providing services to students with disabilities requires a clear understanding of legal responsibilities and procedures, access to state intermediate systems, adequate funding, and instructional capacity.

Charter schools face unique operational challenges associated with their governance structure, size, mission, and newness. A national survey of charter school operators regarding special education documented five big "ongoing challenges" related to charter schools and special education: funding, NCLB requirements, obtaining IEP files, and finding both special education teachers and related services personnel (see table 6.1).

These difficulties (which probably mirror the difficulties facing traditional public schools in this area) potentially influence every aspect of providing special services to children with disabilities. Based on the survey findings and discussions with key informants, we categorized the primary operational challenges as (1) special education capacity, (2) limited resources, (3) shared service delivery, and (4) the balance of autonomy and accountability.[81]

Table 6.1. Ongoing challenges related to charter schools and special education

SPECIAL EDUCATION CHALLENGE	% CHARTER SCHOOL OPERATORS REPORTED
Having adequate funds to provide special education services	58.3%
NCLB requirements related to students with disabilities	54.8%
Obtaining IEP files from sending schools	51.8%
Finding qualified special education teachers	51.7%
Finding qualified related services personnel	46.5%

SOURCE: RHIM, LANGE, AHEARN, AND MCLAUGHLIN (2007A)

81. The impact of these challenges is somewhat dependent on a charter school's legal identity. Charter schools that are independent LEAs generally are required to have greater capacity than charter schools that can rely on their local district for assistance. Depending on their total enrollment, LEA charter schools may or may not be able to realize economies of scale. In turn, charter schools that are part of a district have to navigate shared responsibilities with local districts that may or may not be particularly open to collaborating with the new semi-autonomous schools.

Capacity

Capacity to provide special education is not just a matter of dollars. It also implies having the human resources required to administer and develop a special education program providing a wide array of services. As Ahearn said, "Special education hangs heavily over charter schools. The movement has to acknowledge that this specialized knowledge is needed."

The challenge of building and maintaining special education capacity is not unique to charter schools but charter schools face distinct challenges because they are new, have limited external support, are trying to fulfill a specific mission, and are generally small with a small instructional staff. Frequently, these schools simply do not have the critical mass to support the required special education administrative structure, much less to access high-quality special education personnel. Many we interviewed said that lack of technical knowledge of IDEA contributes to a situation in which charter schools "don't know what they don't know."

Specialized instructional personnel and materials are also essential. Most special education programs employ not only a qualified special education teacher and/or aides, but related services personnel to provide specialized therapies (e.g., occupational, speech, or psychological therapy). Commenting on the challenges of finding qualified personnel, Sneed of SUNY noted, "It is hard to find enough teachers. [What's more,] you need someone with greater breadth and background to support the teachers. This is a serious issue for charter schools."

The struggle to build capacity can be exacerbated by the practical reality that even if they find an administrator or special education teacher who is willing to work part-time, they may not be able to retain the qualified professional due to lack of resources relative to traditional public schools that enjoy economies of scale.

Special education materials are also an issue. Special education programs employ specialized curricula and often require assistive technology devices (e.g., Braille embosser, text-to-Braille conversion, or alternative keyboards). This equipment is inevitably expensive. Giovannetti reflected on the challenge of building capacity:

> At the school level, for general and special education teachers, does the staff have all the tools they need? If they have the knowledge, do they have the materials? If I don't have tools—materials, books, computer programs, and manipulative/assistive technology—or simple things like tables that are small enough to break out in small groups, how do I have capacity?

One of the assets of charter schools in general—their small size—becomes a problem when special education enters the picture. O'Neill of Edison Schools emphasized that the "size of the school really matters." Larger schools simply have a greater opportunity to take advantage of more resources and realize economies of scale. Along these lines, Julie Mead of the University of Wisconsin noted, "Charter schools may not have the capacity to weather the shortage of special education staff. This may be harder in the charter setting by virtue of the size." O'Neill also observed that many of the issues that plagued what he referred to as "early or first generation" schools have been addressed in "second generation" schools that benefit from the experience of authorizers and better developed state, regional, and national networks. Sneed of SUNY's Charter Schools Institute noted that lack of affiliation with a partner such as a charter or education management organization also contributes to the capacity issue: "If you are a mom-and-pop [i.e., independent new start-up], it is hard to have a realistic understanding ... to understand what kind of impact special education can have on your school. I have seen it repeatedly."

Numerous informants noted that capacity can be particularly difficult for charter schools that operate as their own LEAs. Smith of the National Alliance for Public Charter Schools explained, "If they don't do it right, they are particularly vulnerable if they are an LEA due to liability that could destroy the school." And, O'Neill pointed out, "If the school is their own LEA, the challenges are going to be significant. Responsibility is unmitigated for LEAs. It can have a dampening effect for potential developers."

Lack of capacity can cause changes in behavior that lead to charter schools violating special education law. For instance, if a charter school cannot afford to hire qualified speech therapists, they may not adequately deliver this service as prescribed on a student's IEP. Lack of capacity may also lead to "inclusion" in the general-education classroom (normally considered a positive approach) without adequate aids and supports (potentially educationally destructive). Charter operators have reported that the inability to realize "economies of scale" can limit their ability to provide adequate special education services.[82]

Lack of capacity or perceived lack of capacity can lead to charter schools advising parents of students with disabilities against enrolling their child in the school. If a charter school is part of a local district, this advice is arguably permissible if discussed within the confines of an IEP meeting. However, if the advice is offered by charter schools functioning as independent districts, it would be inappropriate counseling out and not in compliance with IDEA.

---

82. Ahearn et al., 2001; Lange, Rhim and Ahearn, 2008.

Limited Special Education Dollars

Funds matter everywhere and they make a difference in charter schools too. However, the issue can be particularly problematic for small charter schools with small budgets. There are three parts to this issue: access to resources, the high costs associated with children with disabilities, and challenges around economies of scale.

First is the challenge of access to revenue. The 2006 litigation in Maryland related to the definition of "commensurate" mentioned above[83] illustrates this issue, as does the example from Michigan regarding access to Medicaid dollars. Limited access to revenue can be further compounded if charter school operators do not have a clear understanding of how federal and state special education dollars flow to schools. They may not be aware of what dollars they should be requesting or what funding pools they can tap.

Mary Street of the Massachusetts Department of Education and a former principal of a charter school noted, "Resources are a huge issue ... having enough money. My school had a kid on a Section 504 plan and for a little school, supporting technology can be a huge expense. Resource issues are huge." In their case study of a charter school in Ohio, Carolyn Sullins and Gary Miron quoted a charter school operator regarding the cost of special education:[84]

> We need greater financial resources to hire more staff—aides, full-time speech, more [occupational therapy], and additional special ed. teachers to provide Title 1 services, pull out children on IEPs. We have a disproportionately high number of students who would benefit from receiving special education services and not enough manpower to provide these services.

Already limited resources can be stretched thin by parents who do not inform charter school operators that their child has an IEP in the hopes that a child can drop the label of special education when they enroll in the charter school.[85] A charter school operator from Ohio explained, "Some parents wouldn't sign papers permitting their children to be evaluated ... schools must provide necessary services, but they won't get paid unless parents sign the permission forms."[86] While districts may be able to absorb the costs of failing to identify one or two students (or identifying them after state counts have been provided), small charter schools do not enjoy that luxury.

Second, there is the challenge of expenses associated with children with disabilities. While this challenge is not unique to charter schools, and in fact is

83. *Baltimore City Board of School Commissioners v. City Neighbors Charter School*, 2006.
84. Sullins and Miron, 2005, 117.
85. Ahearn et al., 2001.
86. Sullins and Miron, 2005, 120.

an ongoing issue for many school districts, the proportionate effect of these costs in connection with a single child can be greater for a small charter school than for a district with multiple schools and, consequently, a larger budget. Specialized services that can run upwards of $50,000 to $100,000 annually (or more for private placements) represent a greater percentage of a charter school's budget than most traditional public schools' budgets. The challenges that charter schools face in accessing standard state special education services further limit charter schools' special education spending.

And, of course, both of these challenges interact and compound yet another: the inability to benefit from economies of scale around special education. So, for example, a charter school with one child with autism must provide the same services as a district with a large number of autistic children. Smith of the Alliance explained, "They have the problem of losing economies of scale and cannot get back to scale with quality. How do you do it on your own? If you are an independent, single charter and don't have a co-op, you are cut off from the district. If they send you any staff or resources, it is their most expendable. They don't regard you as part of their business."

Shared Service Delivery

Shared responsibility for special education occurs when a charter school and other entities split responsibility for fulfilling the obligations outlined in IDEA. This occurs when the charter statute requires charter schools to be part of a local district or when charter schools that are designated in a statute as independent opt to partner with another entity for specific or comprehensive services (e.g., contract with a local district or external consulting firm for special education and related services). Shared responsibility can pose notable operational challenges around roles, obligations, and quantity and quality of services.

When required to share responsibility, the charter school and the other entity, most often the local authorizing district, must first determine who is responsible for specific aspects of special education. For instance, if a charter is part of a local district, who is responsible for paying for evaluations? Who leads the IEP team? Who is responsible for ensuring that procedural timelines are followed? If the district assigns special education personnel to the charter school, does the school have the opportunity to assess whether the teacher understands and supports the school's mission? Tensions related to shared responsibilities may also emerge during the referral process should the charter school and the authorizer disagree about the need for a referral or about the extent or type of support required. Negotiating these shared responsibilities can be complicated by animosity between the charter school and the authorizer (especially local district authorizers) that may be hostile to the charter concept.

Beyond that, there is frequently tension regarding service quality and quantity. In most cases, the charter school is at a significant disadvantage when attempting to hold the authorizer accountable for special education services provided.[87] Smith described the dilemma in the following way:

They are caught in a bind of using the same services that caused families to flee from the district or [schools] must go on their own in an uncertain market . . . . What I worry is that you have charter schools that have control over their personnel and get incredible people to work for them and then [hire] some leftover person from the district to provide special education services.

An area where this can be particularly apparent is in the provision of related services such as occupational and speech therapy where there is a notable shortage in the market and districts may already be facing a backlog of requests.

State officials and authorizers are uniquely positioned to attempt to clarify roles and responsibilities, but research indicates that these entities are frequently not aware of how much or how little charter schools know about educating children with disabilities under IDEA and consequently, do not necessarily know what issues need to be outlined in detail.[88] The written charter application and subsequent contract, also commonly referred to as a Memorandum of Understanding, should define in great detail how IDEA is implemented in the charter school,[89] including explicit guidance regarding the actual provision of special education and related services.

Regardless of legal identity or other formal relationships, multiple informants identified the ability of charter school personnel to build professional relationships as critical to charter schools successfully navigating shared responsibilities. As noted by Barnett from the Massachusetts Department of Education, absent solid relationships, "animosity between charter schools and districts can overshadow what is best for the child."

Shared responsibility potentially provides charter schools with access to broad and deep special education support systems. However, successfully managing the day-to-day details of shared service provision requires a functional relationship between the charter school and its authorizer.

---

87. Ahearn et al., 2001.
88. Ibid; Lange et al., 2004.
89. Green and Mead, 2004.

Balancing Autonomy and Accountability

The final operational challenge identified relates to developing innovative charter school special education programs within a high-stakes accountability environment. Some states are reportedly holding charter schools to a higher standard or viewing charter schools as easy targets due to their being new and different. Barnett explained:

> Charter schools suffer from elevated expectations, and are often judged according to a higher standard. Compliance auditors go into these schools expecting them to be perfect simply because they operate on a charter issued by the Department, ignoring the fact that every non-charter public school district in the state is also out of compliance, to some extent.

On a similar note, O'Neill of Edison Schools and formerly an authorizer in New York noted:

> An issue is mis-regulation and overregulation by state and district authorities who take the approach that they are going to come down hard and regulate charters even when the traditional public schools are not getting regulated. This is the 'neck small enough to get your hands around.' Regulators will focus on charter schools because it is easier to deal with the charter school. Their neck is small enough. Special education is one of those things that if you look hard enough you will find an infraction.

Specifically related to special education programming, Barnett noted:

> Innovative practices are sometimes erroneously cited as noncompliance simply because they do not look similar to programs that the auditor has seen before. Therefore, the auditor reckons, there must be something wrong. Yet innovation is essential to the mandate of charter schools, and to penalize them in this manner is a perverse disincentive to improving services to students with disabilities.

As reported by interviewees in Michigan, many traditional systems simply do not know how to respond to new—and, in many cases, different—schools that require the existing system to rethink standard operating procedures, including procedures associated with accountability.

CONCLUSION

Charter schools face multiple procedural and operational challenges that can impede their development of quality special education programs and consequently the degree to which they are viable options for children with disabilities. The list of challenges is long and daunting, including

- lack of understanding of complex special education rules and regulations;

- lack of clarity about the legal responsibilities of charter schools, as independent districts or as part of existing districts;
- lack of access to state special education services and support structures;
- antiquated education statutes that do not recognize the existence of charter schools;
- resistance on the part of existing public school systems to work with new charter schools;
- limited or weak capacity;
- stretched dollars and resources;
- the challenge of negotiating shared service delivery systems; and
- the difficulty of balancing autonomy and accountability.

Cumulatively, these challenges hinder charter schools' efforts to create high-quality special education programs for children with disabilities. But if the challenges are daunting, the opportunities for charter schools in the area of special education are also quite impressive.

Chapter 7

Opportunities for Innovation and Improvement

LAUREN MORANDO RHIM

B y definition, charter schools create an opportunity to develop a new kind of school; by extension, they also create an opportunity to think differently about how to educate students with disabilities. To fully realize the opportunities around students with disabilities, key stakeholders (including state policy leaders, authorizers, charter school developers, and parents) need to operate in a policy environment conducive to new attitudes. They also need to be equipped with technical knowledge about the Individuals with Disabilities Education Act (IDEA) and related state statutes so that they know what is permissible within the confines of these laws.

The emerging literature and discussions with key informants reveal multiple opportunities for charter schools to minimize the challenges associated with educating students with disabilities and capitalize on promising innovations. While we categorize these as policy, research, and investment opportunities, in fact they are, in many ways, the mirror image of several of the challenges outlined in chapter 6.

POLICY OPPORTUNITIES

As noted in the previous chapter, multiple layers of law, regulation, policy, and practice complicate the task of providing special education in charter schools. Four policy changes could greatly improve the environment in which charter schools educate children with disabilities:
- greater clarity in charter statutes,
- equalized special education funding,
- improved access to service and support structures, and
- new incentives for authorizers and operators to collaborate on developing high-quality charter special education programs.

Clarify Legal Status and Responsibilities

Legal responsibilities are not always clear and, even when clear, new charter school operators frequently do not understand the scope of their responsibilities. While a potential solution could be a federal mandate related to the legal identity of charter schools, individual states and authorizers have successfully navigated special education law in both types of charter schools (independent of local education agency [LEA] and charter-as-LEA); it is not clear that either legal status is substantively better than the other.

Rather than pressing for a federal definition of the legal status of charter schools, advocates working in individual states should identify statutory language or related practices that contribute to the confusion regarding legal identity. For example, clearly defining the delegation of roles and responsibilities for charter schools that are part of an LEA and outlining the operational meaning of "proportionate" or "commensurate" funding are examples of obvious policy opportunities. Prior to a charter being awarded, specific guidance should also be developed to outline the roles and responsibilities of authorizers and charter developers with regard to special education. The proposal here is not that certain entities should assume a specific role, but that the assignment of roles should be made in an intentional, thoughtful, and neutral manner.

Equalize Charter School Special Education Funding

Special education funding and inadequate funding is a persistent point of contention in public education. Research has documented that charter schools do not receive commensurate amounts of the already inadequate dollars.[90] At a minimum, policy advocates need to lobby to ensure that the constructs of "commensurate" or "proportionate" are clearly defined and equitable for both traditional public and charter schools alike. For charter schools operating as part of a district, additional clarity is required regarding the services provided using funds pooled at the district central office. If pooled funds are distributed in the form of professional development or services, charter schools may be at a disadvantage.

Increase Access to Service Infrastructures

A third policy opportunity is to address state policy barriers that clearly impede charter schools' provision of special education and related services (e.g., exclusion from participating in cooperatives). As noted in chapter 6, idiosyncratic

---

90. Thomas B. Fordham Institute, 2005.

aspects of state law in many jurisdictions impede charter schools' efforts to build their capacity to provide special education and related services. Targeted advocacy focused on changing or reinterpreting state laws that limit charter schools in the area of special education is required.

Provide Incentives to Develop High-Quality Special Education Programs

A more radical policy opportunity would be to provide incentives to states or authorizers to encourage them to work with charter schools to (1) accelerate shared knowledge of special education and (2) create opportunities for new approaches to providing special education. For instance, state departments of education could establish a competitive grant program that encourages authorizers and charter school operators to collaborate to rethink special education delivery models or reduce the number of children referred to special education by implementing early intervention services. As noted by Barry Barnett of the Massachusetts Department of Education, a key aspect of innovation should be a focus on outcomes for children with disabilities rather than process: "The fact is, we will be forever locked into this hopeless cycle of compliance-oriented, bureaucratic tail-chasing until we evolve a system of special education program evaluation that is based on outcomes rather than paperwork. We can argue about compliance and applicability of regulations forever, but results speak for themselves."

RESEARCH OPPORTUNITIES

The charter school movement also possesses a number of promising research opportunities. While national studies have advanced the discussion about special education in the charter sector, additional research is required to examine special education practice in charter schools and explore new instructional approaches.

Four research opportunities are particularly promising:
- research on referral process, service provision, and outcomes,
- definitions of "least restrictive environment,"
- assessments of academic growth of students with disabilities, and
- identification of new approaches to special education.

Referral Process, Service Provision, and Outcomes

Charter school operators and advocates claim that charter schools are creating programs that enable students with disabilities (1) to be educated *successfully* in less restrictive environments and (2) to avoid being labeled as special education and still receive adequate services. To date, there are very limited data to back up these claims.

These are complex issues, made all the more complicated by the argument that charter schools may be making sure that their special education population matches the percentage in traditional public schools in order to avoid criticism regarding counseling out children with disabilities. While research has documented that some charter schools do in fact counsel children with more severe disabilities not to enroll,[91] there is also some evidence that charter schools are serving students in less restrictive environments (i.e., a greater percentage of their day is spent in general education classrooms).[92]

Overall, we know little about the degree to which the special education referral process and service provision in charter schools is driven by what is appropriate for the child, or conversely, by what is appropriate given the resources and school space and facilities. A study that examines how charter schools manage the pre-referral and referral process to discern whether fewer children are being formally identified along with related analyses of these students' academic progress would provide valuable insights into the process. If such a study identified practices that could, in the long run, decrease the number of students referred into special education, that would be a valuable outcome, not simply for charter schools, but for public schools nationwide.

The most recent Annual Report to Congress on the Implementation of IDEA (2009) examines the "declassification" of elementary school students.[93] An analogous examination of a random sample of charter schools could document or rebut the anecdotal evidence regarding the degree to which charter schools are serving children with disabilities outside of special education. A companion study examining how children with disabilities are educated, and the degree to which their individualized education programs (IEPs) change when they enter charter schools, tied to an analysis of academic outcomes over time, would provide additional insight into the degree to which charter schools effectively educate children in less restrictive environments.

---

91. Rhim, Lange, Ahearn, and McLaughlin, 2007a.

92. Downing et al., 2004; Fiore, et al., 2000; Guarino and Chau, 2003; Rhim, Faukner, and McLaughlin, 2006.

93. U.S. Department of Education, Office of Special Education and Rehabilitative Services, Office of Special Education Programs, 2009.

Explore Least Restrictive Environments

An emerging theme that multiple informants raised, but for which there is no research base, is the issue of "least restrictive environments" in charter schools that are designed primarily, if not entirely, for children with disabilities.

Under state law, charter schools are required to maintain open enrollment policies; the federal Public Charter Program requires schools receiving federal charter school funding to conduct lotteries if they are over-enrolled. In that context, a small but growing niche in the charter sector consists of special education schools. There are currently more than 70 charter schools with a mission explicitly oriented to primarily serving students with disabilities.[94] Such schools are not permitted to discriminate in enrollment decisions against children who do not have disabilities, although they are perfectly free to promote themselves as specializing in instructional approaches that will be particularly appealing to a relatively small minority of students. They might, for example, be schools for children with autism or schools for the deaf.

Advocates for these schools argue that they allow for a highly individualized learning environment. A study of the schools found that they were established by (1) teachers who wanted to use a particular instructional approach, (2) parents who wanted to expand the options available to their children, and (3) existing programs that served individuals with disabilities.[95] Special education advocates question the degree to which a school that in practice only enrolls students with one particular disability can offer adequate exposure to peers without disabilities, that is to say, meet the least restrictive environment standard. Yet, parents who elect to send their children to these specialized programs are making the choice, presumably based on their knowledge of their child.

Charter schools that specialize in programs for children with specific disabilities are controversial due to the debates surrounding "least restrictive environment" and may face judicial intervention in the future. Special education legal scholar Julie Mead from the University of Wisconsin questions the degree to which special education charter schools represent the least restrictive environment; she worries that they may develop a "vested interest in retaining the population and putting their stamp of approval on parents' choice."[96] Mead notes that when children enroll in charter schools primarily or entirely for children with disabilities, they may lose the "checks and balances" that ideally characterize IEP meetings.[97]

---

94. Mead, 2007
95. Ibid.
96. Ibid.
97. Ibid.

The overarching question related to least restrictive environment is "What kind of environment is best for individual children academically, socially, and emotionally?" Rigorous empirical research that examines the potential merits of developing special education focused charter schools and, specifically, how students fare in these schools compared to other settings is required. By allowing for the development of different models, coupled with parental choice, the charter sector has opened up new research issues that may benefit both charter and traditional public schools.

Assess Academic Growth of Students with Disabilities

Research on the achievement of students with disabilities in charter schools is so far inconclusive. A 2003 study documented that students in California charter schools scored the same as or below their peers in traditional public schools.[98] But a 2006 analysis comparing academic outcomes of students with disabilities enrolled in traditional versus charter schools found higher levels of proficiency for those students enrolled in charter schools.[99]

Clearly these differing findings call for further investigation. To determine the relative effects of charter schools on the academic performance of students with disabilities, one must examine individual student growth or change in achievement over time. The use of growth models that measure change in performance within schools should allow states to track more precisely the achievement levels of students with disabilities who enroll in charter schools, as well as to examine the performance of charter schools compared to that of traditional public schools. In line with recommendations regarding rigorous examination of charter school student achievement in general, research efforts will need to navigate the pitfalls of this kind of analysis and should follow the guidance of the National Charter School Research Project's consensus panel on the topic.[100]

Identify New Approaches to Special Education

The opportunity to create a new school includes the potential to rethink how to deliver special education absent standard operating practices. For children with disabilities receiving specialized services in a highly regulated environment, these services may be based more on routine than rigorous research.

---

98. Guarino and Chau, 2003.

99. Rhim, Faukner, and McLaughlin, 2006.

100. For a more extensive discussion of the consensus panel, see: http://www.ncsrp.org/cs/csr/view/initiatives/2.

Research aimed at identifying and examining break-the-mold special education practices in charter schools is required. The practices need to be documented, evaluated, and—if justified—disseminated. For instance, multiple interviewees noted that charter schools that have developed successful programs, including programs for children with disabilities, embrace a fundamental commitment to serve all students. Elizabeth Giovannetti noted: "The charter schools making [Annual Yearly Progress (AYP)] embrace a philosophy that all students can learn. That is their belief and that is what they exude in their building. Kids feel that energy and truly believe that they can succeed." This philosophical belief is reportedly infused into the school culture so that special education is not a separate stand-alone program, but rather an integrated component of a successful instructional program.[101] Multiple interviewees noted that good instruction is good for all children, including children with disabilities. The schools that develop successful programs to reflect the commitment to educate all children need to be examined to determine what lessons can be culled for the broader educational community.

INVESTMENT OPPORTUNITIES

The informants consulted during the course of developing this report identified multiple opportunities to invest in systems or support structures to help charter schools address the multiple challenges involved with special education. Five potentially fruitful investment opportunities were identified:
- incubating technical assistance networks,
- charter-specific special education service structures,
- seeding special education financial risk pools,
- funding efforts to maximize special education revenue streams, and
- developing legal advocacy funds for charter schools.

Incubate Technical Assistance Networks

Stakeholders recognize that extensive technical assistance is required to build the special education capacity for state agencies, authorizers, and charter school operators. The lack of knowledge and experience, particularly among state department of education personnel, inexperienced authorizers, and new charter operators, is a crucial underlying factor fueling the multiple special education challenges. The National Association of State Directors of Special Education has devoted considerable attention to educating state directors of special education and authorizers about charter schools but more work is required to ensure that state-level

---

101. Downing, Spencer, and Cavallaire, 2004.

personnel (e.g., curriculum specialists, financial analysts, and auditors) understand where charter schools fit within the state educational landscape. From the other end of the spectrum, charter school authorizers and operators need training to understand the scope of responsibilities related to IDEA and to ensure that charter applicants and operators understand the many requirements.

Mandating training or requiring specific levels of knowledge are approaches that are typically resisted by charter operators, who tend to oppose regulation. Still, state education agencies, authorizers, and state charter organizations are uniquely positioned to provide substantive up-front training and technical assistance during the application phase and after charters have been granted.[102] The emerging network of technical assistance providers (e.g., charter school associations, charter school resource centers, local nonprofits, charter management organizations, and education management organizations) in cooperation with existing traditional special education service infrastructures are logical investment opportunities.

Multiple states have developed charter-specific special education technical assistance networks. Minnesota developed the Minnesota Charter School Special Education Project; Michigan launched the Vision for a New Way with support from its state Department of Education. Other states and charter school authorizers allocate dollars to help special education professionals provide technical assistance to charter schools (e.g., Colorado Charter Schools Institute and the Massachusetts Department of Education).

Officials at the Massachusetts Department of Education have suggested a charter school special education hotline operated by a qualified special education administrator. The administrator would be available to help charter schools with day-to-day operational issues. With the proliferation of Internet-based communication and collaboration tools, more high-tech solutions that use the Internet to connect schools with human technical assistance providers are increasingly feasible. In addition, web platforms are ideal for developing and sharing knowledge bases so that practitioners do not have to reinvent the wheel. Investments in these kinds of virtual support for charter school special education programs could yield new models for helping special educators in all settings.

Charter-Specific Special Education Service Structures

Early research on special education in the charter sector identified the need for charter schools to access special education service support systems. Charter schools, like traditional public schools, need the support of an infrastructure to help them address the myriad administrative and programmatic responsibilities

---

102. Rhim, Lange, Ahearn, and McLaughlin, 2007a; Rhim, Lange, Ahearn, and McLaughlin, 2007b.

> "When [charter schools] are hooked into an infrastructure, they are better prepared to hit the ground running. They can tap into economics of scale and they have a network to tap into when they have questions."
>
> —*Julie Mead, University of Wisconsin*

involved with special education. These support structures (whether internal or external) typically provide schools with the human, fiscal, legal, and organizational capacity to meet requirements associated with providing a free and appropriate public education.[103]

While a support structure may provide some technical assistance, a service structure engages in *ongoing provision* of direct special education and related services. Entities providing special education infrastructure support to charter schools include local districts, intermediate administrative units (e.g., intermediate school districts, education services centers, and boards of cooperative education services), cooperatives, local nonprofits, and management organizations.[104] To the outsider they may all look alike; however, Dan Quisenberry of the Michigan Charter Schools Association stressed that "cooperatives are a more attractive option than intermediate districts. Intermediate districts are highly regulated and responsibilities are dictated by the legislature. Charter schools started because of a desire to do things differently. Cooperatives give charter schools the options to do things differently."

Investments in charter-specific special education support structures could take the form of state competitive grant programs for organizations interested in creating such entities. Charter schools could also engage philanthropic organizations to provide seed money to existing charter support organizations (e.g., associations or resource centers) to facilitate the creation of charter school special education cooperatives. Special education cooperatives, in which multiple schools voluntarily pool their resources, were identified by nearly all of the key informants as promising strategies to build charter schools' special education capacity.

While informants find the idea attractive, to date, few cities or states can point to operating charter school special education cooperatives. It may be the case that beyond the need for members of a cooperative to be geographically proximate, it is hard to find the time required to carefully organize and manage a cooperative, not to mention creating the procedures to ensure that all members not only have a voice but also see the value of pooling their resources.

---

103. Ahearn et al., 2001.

104. Rhim, Lange, Ahearn, and McLaughlin, 2006.

Given the widespread success of cooperatives in the traditional public school sector, these entities hold promise in the charter sector but thoughtful investment in capacity-building is required.

One fruitful investment strategy might be to identify existing special education service support structures that are working well and encourage them to scale up to serve other cities and states. Organizations with strong leadership, a proven track record, and existing systems provide a solid platform from which to reach more charter schools, rather than starting from scratch. Due to variations in state and local policy, of course, a scale-up operation would need to adapt the initial model to new settings. Where scale-up is not possible, investors could consider backing the start-up of new cooperatives.

Another possible approach to increasing special education service infrastructures would be to invest in existing human resource pipelines that would expand the number of qualified special education administrators and teachers available to work in charter schools. For instance, investors could support a specialized charter school administrator training program through New Leaders for New Schools or a teacher training program through The New Teacher Project.

Seed Special Education Financial Risk Pools

Special education risk pools are a specific type of special education infrastructure. Unlike infrastructures that provide human and organizational services, a financial risk pool focuses solely on pooling special education dollars to be drawn on as needed when contributing schools or districts are faced with purchasing high-cost special education services. IDEA (2004) includes language encouraging the creation of state special education risk pools by authorizing states to reserve up to 10 percent of their state-level activities funds to "to establish and make disbursements from the high cost fund to LEAs" and to "support innovative and effective ways of cost sharing by the state, by an LEA or among a consortium of LEAs, as determined by the state in coordination with representatives from LEAs."[105]

An initial infusion of funds, which could be in the form of a loan or "program related investment," could capitalize a risk pool. Thereafter, member charter schools would pay annual insurance-like premiums into the pool and, in return, could make claims on the pool if they enrolled students who require particular high-cost services. Like any insurance pool, charter school special education risk pools would require thoughtful design to ensure that they do not create perverse incentives and are financially sustainable past involvement of the original founders. The state of Colorado has operated a special education

---

105. *Individuals with Disabilities Education Act of 2004.*

insurance model for a number of years and research has documented its positive aspects.[106] However, the model was not voluntary and charter schools had limited control of its conditions. A risk pool created and managed by charter school partners has the potential to prepare a charter school to manage the potential heavy financial costs of a child who requires intensive services. Such a risk pool would also diminish the incentive to counsel out children with greater special education needs.

Maximize Access to Revenue Streams

While special education dollars fall short of individual schools' needs, charter schools are not accessing all potential sources of revenue. Funds allocated to helping a group of charter schools maximize their revenue stream could boost schools' ability to build special education capacity. For example, a valuable task tackled by the original founders of the Washington, D.C., special education cooperative was navigating Medicaid rules and regulations to identify funds charter schools were eligible to receive based on who they were educating. A secondary benefit would be identifying students enrolled in charter schools who are eligible to receive Medicaid funds. Navigating cumbersome Medicaid policies and procedures would have been overwhelming for any single school administrator. A centralized group supported by multiple charter schools can benefit all of them.

Medicaid is just one example of a potential funding stream. There may be other special education dollars or more general health and youth funding streams that an enterprising, focused effort could tap for charters—funds that traditional districts may already access.

Create Legal Advocacy Funds

Due in part to lack of clarity associated with interpreting multiple layers of policy, charter school advocates have had to engage the legal system to clarify charter school issues in general, as well as issues pertaining to special education.[107] Litigation is expensive and ideally used only as a last resort. Nevertheless, a tangible investment in addressing special education challenges is a legal defense fund. To date, four states (California, Colorado, Florida, and New Mexico) have created formal, multiple-purpose charter school legal funds. These funds have helped support charter schools or parents fight for reinterpretation of state charter laws. Examples of issues that states have litigated to date involve

---

106. Ahearn et al., 2001.
107. O'Neill, Wenning, and Giovannetti, 2002.

transportation for a child with a disability who chose to attend a charter school and the definition of "commensurate" or "proportionate" funding for children in charter schools, including children with disabilities.

A fund set aside for charter school legal advocacy could provide both charter schools and parents of children in charter schools with a centralized means to improve existing local and state policies. Discussions with charter advocates revealed that, since most charter school issues pertain to local interpretation of state rules and regulations and because the entities most invested in changing policies are local, legal advocacy funds for the most part are best organized by state. For example, in Colorado, the legal fund is based at the Colorado League of Charter Schools. Yet, given that most special education policy originates from the federal statute, there may be a place for a national charter school legal fund should a case emerge that raises constitutional issues such as issues related to due process and equal protection.

CONCLUSION

In brief, it is clear that many opportunities exist to expand the potential of charter schools to educate students with disabilities. They revolve around policy, research, and investment. Advocates, foundations, and state and federal officials should consider these opportunities carefully because, as this volume makes clear, many charter schools are doing outstanding work educating children with disabilities.

Chapter 8

Summary and Discussion

ROBIN J. LAKE

To restate the point made at the outset of this volume, this book addresses choices made at the intersection of two very important policy arenas in education: special education and charter schools—unique students and unique schools to serve them.

In a very real sense, this volume also underscores the central theme of *Hopes, Fears, & Reality 2008*, the annual review of charter school issues published by the Center on Reinventing Public Education's National Charter School Research Project: charter school programs for students with special needs are, like charter schools themselves, more different than alike.

Some focus on academic skills, others on social and emotional development. While one charter school will aim to prepare students for college, another will try to make sure its graduates are employment-ready the minute they graduate. Perhaps the most significant difference of all is that some charter schools mainstream students with disabilities, while others specialize in serving students with particular kinds of disabilities, often very severe special needs. In brief, as with public education generally, practically any statement about charter schools (and special-needs students in charter schools) is likely to be true somewhere, and no generalization about charter schools will be true everywhere.

Against that backdrop, this small volume begins to fill in a major hole in charter school research. It has been developed for the education generalist. It does not begin to do justice to the three major sets of papers from which these chapters were drawn. We urge readers to turn to the originals for more detailed discussions of methodology and school approaches. What this volume does do is provide a solid working foundation for readers interested in charter schools and special education. It explores how parents choose schools for their children with special needs. It describes what we know about both the legal requirements for special education and what those requirements imply for charter schools. It describes how charter schools that seem to serve students with special needs especially well attempt to meet those needs, as well as those of all their students.

In this volume, we learn, for example, that:

Charter schools are governed by the same federal special education laws as other public schools, but interpretation of those laws is not always clear

A series of federal enactments dating back to Title VI of the Elementary and Secondary Education Act of 1965, backed up by federal and state court decisions, provide relatively unambiguous guidance for all public schools, including charter schools.

- Charter schools are required by statute to adhere to all the civil rights guarantees laid out in the Individuals with Disabilities Education Act (IDEA), including those insisting on "a free and appropriate public education" in the "least restrictive environment" through an "individualized education program" (IEP).
- Responding to onerous federal and state statutes and regulations around special education is a challenge for all schools, traditional and charter alike.
- Charter schools' legal environment is potentially even more complicated than that of the typical public school, based on whether the charter school is part of a local education agency (LEA) (which assumes responsibility for meeting state regulations governing special education) or are their own LEA (in which case the charter school assumes LEA responsibility).

The average charter school enrolls a slightly smaller proportion of students with disabilities than do public schools overall (10.6 percent versus 11.51 percent). However, it is not clear that these average percentages are particularly meaningful on their face. One reason is that individual school special-needs populations vary greatly under both charter and district governance, so the average numbers mask important school level differences. There are surely some charter schools that "counsel out" students with special needs, and this is cause for concern, but this is also the case in many district-run public schools. It is also likely that at least some charter schools are reporting smaller proportions of children with disabilities because they are providing effective early interventions or offering an educational program that reduces the need to label children. It may also be that parents of students with more severe disabilities are satisfied with their district schools and less likely to seek an alternative.

At least in California, charter schools also seem to enroll a greater proportion of students with high-incidence disabilities, such as learning disabilities, than do traditional public schools (61 percent of students with learning disabilities vs. 55 percent). Families of these students may be most likely to seek out the smaller, more personalized environments that charter schools are known for.

Parents do not see charters as a panacea for their children with special needs, but they are often an important alternative

Parents have little ideological interest in which school is best for their child; they have a desperate need to find the best fit. The parents of children with special needs look very much like parents of typical children in the information sources they use in making school choice decisions. However, parents of children with special needs view their children as fragile, and susceptible to greater damage if the wrong school is chosen. As a result, the school choice process seems to be even more focused on the needs of the individual child, and parents continue to monitor the school closely to make sure that initial expectations and ongoing needs are met. Parents feel that no one will advocate for their child as strongly as they will. They also understand that the needs of their child and the financial pressures experienced by schools and districts are often at odds. This is exhausting and frustrating for many parents.

Because of the highly individualized nature of this process, differences across schools are more important to the parents of children with special needs than are more general differences between charter schools and traditional public schools. Whether they attend charter schools or traditional public schools, parents want schools that accept and care about their children, that both challenge and support their children, and that work with parents as active and respected partners in the ongoing education of their children.

Despite the difficulties inherent in maneuvering legal and financial special education requirements within an autonomous school structure, charter schools are viable options for a large number of families with special-needs students. In fact, some charter schools have developed informal reputations as havens for students with special needs. In many cases, particularly with respect to the needs of students with less severe disabilities, the variety of instructional approaches offered by charter schools can serve as beneficial interventions for these students. Effective inclusion for students with less severe needs is a particular strength of many charter schools.

Many parents of children with special needs find what they seek in traditional public schools, but a substantial number increasingly seek out a charter school alternative. The alternatives are not always perfect, but many parents report that despite ongoing difficulties they feel the smaller charter school environment is more appropriate for their children and that they have a greater say in their children's educational program.

Exploratory case studies reveal that effective charter special education programs have many things in common

Six case studies of charter schools with strong reputations and track records reveal broad characteristics and practices that may contribute to strong instructional programs for children with disabilities.

1) Schoolwide commitment to meet individual student needs
- Leadership and, specifically, a core commitment to incorporating children with disabilities in the overall school program
- A common sense of ownership and responsibility among general education teachers and school leadership for the academic performance of all of their students, including students with disabilities
- A commitment to the tenets of IDEA beyond basic compliance and embracing the spirit of the law to provide meaningful and inclusive services to students with disabilities

2) Effective professional supports for teachers
- Targeted and relevant professional development to support meaningful access to the general education curriculum for children with disabilities
- Early intervention and highly individualized instruction based on diagnostic data

3) Customized student interventions and services
- Highly individualized programs for *all* students, general and special education alike, that "normalize" special education in general and the IEP in particular
- Best instructional practices for children *without* disabilities benefit children *with* disabilities and, conversely, interventions typically noted in IEPs (e.g., written directions, assistance with organizational skills, behavioral modification, and redirection) benefit students *without* disabilities

4) A focus on effective instructional strategies over IEP status

5) Safe and respectful student-to-student interactions
These practices are, no doubt, in part due to the fact that these schools are organized as charter schools and are free from many state and local constraints. Our analysis, however, reveals that district public schools should pay attention to these schools and not simply dismiss them as anomalies. Much if not all of what the schools highlighted in this volume are doing can be replicated in

other schools, charter or not. Doing it well, however, will likely require districts to ensure all schools have

- leadership that is receptive to change and committed to educating children with diverse and special needs within one building, and
- adequate funding to train and support teachers and special education personnel to work in profoundly new ways.

The legal framework of special education provides many challenges for charter schools

Despite the success stories we present from the field, many charter schools face many of the same challenges in offering special education that plague traditional public schools. For example, charter schools struggle to hire and retain qualified special education and related services personnel, to understand the plethora of procedural requirements, and to develop high-quality programs with limited resources.

Small stand-alone charter schools may not fully understand their legal responsibilities and may have limited access to technical assistance or special education service providers. There are also significant policy challenges related to charter schools and special education: funding, *No Child Left Behind* requirements, obtaining IEP files, and finding both special education teachers and related services personnel.

But it is equally true that special education provides charter schools with opportunities

Despite the challenges, charter schools and people interested in supporting the sector can also find a number of opportunities around special education.

The first opportunities arise in the policy *area:*
- Clarify legal status and responsibilities in vague laws or regulations
- Equalize charter school special education funding
- Create better oversight and incentives for charter schools to develop high-quality special education

The next lie in the area of research:
- Examine special education service provision and outcomes in charter sector
- Explore definition of "least restrictive environment" in school choice context
- Assess academic growth of children with disabilities in charter schools
- Identify new approaches to special education

The third set of opportunities revolves around needed investments:

- Incubate national, state, and regional technical assistance networks
- Cultivate special education infrastructures (e.g., special education cooperatives) and research tracking effectiveness and financial sustainability
- Seed special education financial risk pools
- Fund efforts to maximize special education revenue streams
- Develop legal advocacy funds for charter schools

DISCUSSION

Educating children with special needs can be an expensive and legally complex endeavor, one that not all small, stand-alone charter schools have handled effectively. This volume begins to build the empirical evidence about how charter schools can navigate the special education policy environment. It explores

- which special education challenges seriously impact the growth and expansion of the charter school movement;
- why parents with special-needs children choose (or do not choose) charter schools;
- practices that charter schools have adopted that could be considered innovative and especially promising for the traditional public education system; and
- the policy, research, and investment opportunities that could best address special education challenges in charter schools.

It also shows that despite the difficulties, there are several outstanding examples of charter schools successfully meeting the challenge of providing special education services to children with special needs. And it suggests that for many parents of students with disabilities, charter schools are a very important option for their children.

By freeing charter schools from restrictions such as (1) how they may choose and arrange their staffs, (2) what curricula and instructional strategies they can adopt, and (3) what financial and staff development priorities they can establish for themselves, policymakers hoped that schools would find more productive approaches to educating all students, including those with unique needs or disabilities. They also hoped that effective new approaches developed in charter schools would eventually be adopted by all public schools. For families of special-needs students, the hope is that a more diverse array of offerings inspired by school choice will provide a greater array of public school options and allow them to find the right fit for their child, whose urgent needs may not be easily understood by a simple label or diagnosis.

This volume brings new evidence and insights to inform—and hopefully help people achieve—these aspirations. There is clearly a lot of work to be done, however, and throughout this volume the contributors provide examples of ongoing research that is needed as well as the policy attention and technical supports required to promote more widespread adoption of the practices we see in effective charter schools.

Until now, most of the policy discussion and even general public discussion about charter schools and special education has revolved around concerns over whether public schools not run directly by a school board would protect the rights of students with special needs. As the charter sector has matured, it seems that charter school personnel are becoming more sophisticated about their legal responsibilities while their public authorizing agencies become more sophisticated about proper accountability and oversight roles. We think it is now time for discussion to turn to how more students with special needs, whether in charter or non-charter public schools, can benefit from high-quality teaching and learning environments.

References

Ahearn, E. A., C. M., Lange, L. M. Rhim, and M. J. McLaughlin. 2001. *Project SEARCH: Special education as requirements in charter schools.* Alexandria, VA: National Association of State Directors of Special Education. Available at http://www.nasdse.org/project_search_doc2.pdf.

Ahearn, E. A., L. M. Rhim, C. M. Lange, and M. J. McLaughlin. 2005. *Project Intersect research report #1: State legislative review.* College Park: University of Maryland, Institute for the Study of Exceptional Children and Youth, Project Intersect.

Andrews, J. E., D. W. Carnine, M. J. Coutinho, E. B. Edgar, S. R. Forness, L. S. Fuchs, D. Jordan, D., Kauffman, J. M. Patton, J. Paul, J. Rosell, R. Rueda, E. Schiller, T. M. Skrtic, and J. Wong. 2000. Bridging the special education divide. *Remedial and Special Education* 21(5): 258-260, 267.

Arsen, D., D. N. Plank, and G. Sykes. 1999. *School choice policies in Michigan: The rules matter.* East Lansing, MI: Michigan State University.

Blackorby, J., and M. Wagner. 1996. Longitudinal postschool outcomes of youth with disabilities: Findings from the National Longitudinal Transition Study. *Exceptional Children* 62(5): 399-413.

Baltimore City Board of School Commissioners v. City Neighbors Charter School, No. 100, September Term. 2006. Available at caselaw.findlaw.com/data2/marylandstatecases/coa/2007/100a06.pdf.

Buckley, J., and M. Schneider. 2006. Are charter school parents more satisfied with schools? Evidence from Washington, DC. *Peabody Journal of Education* 81(1): 57-78.

California Education Code, Section §47645. Available at http://www.leginfo.ca.gov/cgi-bin/displaycode?section=edc&group=47001-48000&file=47640-47647.

California Department of Education. 2007. *California State Board of Education, July 2007 agenda: Item #38.* Available at http://www.cde.ca.gov/be/ag/ag/yr07/documents/july07item38.doc.

Center for Education Reform. 2007. *National charter school data: 2007-2008 new school estimates.* Washington, DC: Center for Education Reform. Available at http://www.edreform.com/_upload/CER_charter_numbers.pdf.

Charter School Achievement Consensus Panel, National Charter School Research Project, http://www.ncsrp.org/cs/csr/view/initiatives/2.

Christensen, J., and R. Lake. 2007. The national charter school landscape in 2007. In *Hopes, fears, & reality: A balanced look at American charter schools in 2007,* ed. R. Lake. National Charter School Research Project. Seattle: Center on Reinventing Public Education.

Colorado Department of Education, Schools of Choice Unit. 2008. *Fall 2007 charter school pupil membership by district and school.* Available at http://www.cde.state.co.us/cdechart/download/chart_enr_2007.pdf.

Colorado Department of Education. 2007. *Fall 2007 pupil membership by county, district, and instructional program.* Available at http://www.cde.state.co.us/cdereval/download/PDF/2007PM/District/DistIPST.pdf.

Commonwealth of Massachusetts, General Laws of Massachusetts, 2006. *Part I. Administration of the government. Title VII. Cities, towns and districts. Chapter 40. Powers and duties of cities and towns. Chapter 40: Section 4E. Education collaboratives.* Available at http://www.mass.gov/legis/laws/mgl/40-4e.htm.

Consoletti, A. 2008. *2008 Charter school laws at-a-glance: Current rankings from first to worst.* Washington, DC: Center for Education Reform. Available at http://www.edreform.com/_upload/ranking_chart.pdf.

DeSchryver, K. 2006. *The state of charter schools in Colorado 2004-05.* Denver, CO: Colorado Department of Education.

Downing, J. E., S. Spencer, and C. Cavallaire (2004). The development of an inclusive charter elementary school: Lessons learned. *Research & Practice for Persons with Severe Disabilities* 29, (1): 11-24.

Duncan-Poitier, J. 2007. 2005–06 *Annual report on the status of charter schools in New York State.* Albany, New York Department of Education, 52.

Estes, M. B. 2000. Charter schools and students with special needs: How well do they mix? *Education and Treatment of Children* 23(3): 369-80.

Finn, C. E., B. V. Manno, and L. A. Bierlein. 1996. *Charter schools in action: What have we learned?* Washington, DC: Hudson Institute.

Finn C. E., B. V. Manno, and G. Vanourek. 2000. *Charter schools in action.* Princeton, NJ: Princeton University Press.

Fiore, T.A., L. M. Harwell, J. Blackorby, and K. S. Finnigan. 2000. *Charter schools and students with disabilities: A national study.* Washington, DC: U.S. Department of Education, Office of Educational Research and Improvement.

Fiore, T. A., and E. R. Cashman. 1998. *Review of charter school legislation provisions related to students with disabilities.* Washington, DC: U.S. Department of Education, Office of Educational Research and Improvement.

Fiore, T. A., S. H. Warren, and E. R. Cashman. 1998. *Charter schools and students with disabilities: Review of existing data.* Washington, DC: U.S. Department of Education, Office of Educational Research and Improvement.

Goodlad, J. 1984. *A place called school.* New York: McGraw-Hill.

Guarino, C., and D. Chau. 2003. Special education in charter and conventional public schools. In *Charter school operations and performance: Evidence from California*, eds. R. Zimmer, R. Buddin, D. Chau, G. Daley, D. Guarino, L. Hamilton, C. Krop, D. McCaffrey, M. Sandler, and D. Brewer. Santa Monica, CA: RAND Education.

Green, P. C., and J. F. Mead. 2004. *Charter schools and the law: Chartering new legal relationships.* Norwood, MA: Christopher-Gordon Publishers.

Herrold, K., and K. O'Donnell. 2008. *Parent and family involvement in education survey 2006-07 school year, from the national household education surveys program of 2007* (NCES 2008-0050). Washington, DC: U.S. Department of Education, National Center for Education Statistics.

Heubert, J. P. 1997. Schools without rules? Charter schools, federal disability law, and the paradoxes of deregulation. *Harvard Civil Rights-Civil Liberties Law Review* 32: 301–353.

Individuals with Disabilities Education Improvement Act of 2004, U.S. Code Title 20, §611(e)(3)(A), Chapter 33—Education of Individuals with Disabilities, as amended by P. L. 108-466.

Johnson, J., and A. Duffett. 2002. *When it's your own child: a report on special education from the families who use it.* New York: Public Agenda.

Kellogg, S., and K. Kafer. 2007. *2006 Special education services in charter schools: Surveying perceptions of charter school administrators and special education directors.* Denver, CO: Colorado Department of Education.

Lake, J. F., and B. S. Billingsley. 2000. An analysis of factors that contribute to parent-school conflict in special education. *Remedial and Special Education*, 21: 4, 240-251.

Lake, R., ed. 2008. *Hopes, fears, & reality: A balanced look at American charter schools in 2008.* National Charter School Research Project. Seattle: Center on Reinventing Public Education.

Lange, C. M. 1997. *School choice, charter schools, and students with disabilities.* Paper presented at the meeting of the American Educational Research Association, Chicago, March, 1997.

Lange, C. M., E. A. Ahearn, E. Giovanetti, L. M. Rhim, and S. Waren. 2004. *Primer for charter school state officials: Special education requirements and including students with disabilities in charter schools.* Available at http://www.uscharterschools.org/specialedprimers/download/state_off_primer.pdf

Lange, C. M., L. M. Rhim, and E. A. Ahearn. 2008. Special education in charter schools: The view from state education agencies. *Journal of Special Education Leadership,* 21: 1, 12-21.

Lange, C. M., L. M. Rhim, E. A. Ahearn, and M. J. McLaughlin. 2005. *Project Intersect research report #2: Survey of state directors of special education.* College Park: University of Maryland, Institute for the Study of Exceptional Children and Youth, Project Intersect.

Lange, C. M., and C. A. Lehr. 2000. Charter schools and students with disabilities: Parent perceptions of reasons for transfer and satisfaction with services. *Remedial and Special Education* 21(3): 141-151.

Maryland Public Charter School Act of 2003. SB 75, Chapter 358 of 2003 Laws of Maryland. Section 9-101, et seq., of the Education Article, Annotated Code of Maryland.

McCully, D., and M. Malin. 2003. *What parents think of New York's charter schools.* Civic report no. 37. New York: Manhattan Institute.

McKinney, J. R., 1996. Charter schools: A new barrier for children with disabilities. *Education Leadership,* 54(2): 22–25.

McKinney, J. R. and J. F. Mead. 1996. Law and policy in conflict: Including students with disabilities in parental-choice programs. *Educational Administrative Quarterly,* 32(1): 107-141.

McLaughlin, M. J., and K. Henderson. 1998. Charter schools in Colorado and their response to the education of students with disabilities. *Journal of Special Education,* 32(2): 99–107.

Mead, J. F. 1995. Including students with disabilities in parental choice programs: The challenge of meaningful choice. *West's Education Law Reporter,* 101 (2): 463-496.

-------. 2007. *Charter schools designed for children with disabilities: An initial examination of issues and questions raised.* Alexandria, VA: National Association of State Directors of Special Education. Availabe at www.uscharterschools.org/specialedprimers.

-------. 2008. *Charter schools designed for children with disabilities: An initial examination of issues and questions raised.* Alexandria, VA: National Association of State Directors of Special Education.

Medler, A., and J. Nathan. 1995. *Charter schools: What are they up to?* Denver, CO: Education Commission of the States.

Miron, G., and C. Nelson. 2002. *What's public about charter schools? Lessons learned about choice and accountability.* Thousand Oaks, CA: Corwin Press.

National Council on Disability. 2008. *The No Child Left Behind Act and the Individuals with Disabilities Education Act: A progress report.* Washington, DC: National Council on Disability.

National Institute on Deafness and Other Communication Disorders. 2009. *Cochlear implants.* Available at http://www.nidcd.nih.gov/health/hearing/coch.asp.

Newman, L. 2005. *Parents' satisfaction with their children's schooling: Facts from OSEP's national longitudinal studies. Ideas that work, June 2005.* Washington, DC: U.S. Department of Education, Office of Special Education Programs.

O'Brien, T., K. Hupfeld, and P. Teske. 2008. *Challenges and charter schools: How families with special-needs students perceive and use charter school options.* NCSRP working paper #2008-10. Seattle: Center on Reinventing Public Education.

O'Neill, P. T., R. J. Wenning, and B. Giovannetti. 2002. Serving students with disabilities in charter schools: Legal obligations and policy options. *169 West's Education Law Reporter 1*. Available at http://www.naschools.org/uploadedfiles/ServingStudentswDisabiltiiesin%20Charter.pdf.

Parker, W. C. 2005. Teaching against idiocy. *Phi Delta Kappan* 86(5): 344–51.

President's Commission on Excellence in Special Education. 2002. *A new era: Revitalizing special education for children and their families.* Washington, DC: U.S. Department of Education. Available at http://www.ed.gov/inits/commissionsboards/whspecialeducation/reports/images/Pres_Rep.pdf.

Renzulli, J. S., and S. M. Reis. 1985. *The schoolwide enrichment model.* Mansfield Center, Connecticut: Creative Learning Press. Executive summary available at http://www.gifted.uconn.edu/sem/semexec.html.

Rhim, L. M. 2008. *Special education challenges and opportunities in the charter school sector.* NCSRP working paper #2008-12. Seattle: Center on Reinventing Public Education.

Rhim, L. M., E. A. Ahearn, and C. M. Lange. 2007. Toward a more sophisticated analysis of the charter school sector: Considering legal identity as a critical variable of interest. *Journal of School Choice* 1(3).

Rhim L. M., and D. Brinson. 2008. *Exploring success in the charter sector: Case studies of six charter schools engaged in promising practices for children with disabilities.* NCSRP working paper #2008-11. Seattle: Center on Reinventing Public Education. Available at: http://www.crpe.org/cs/crpe/download/csr_files/wp_ncsrp11_pubimpact_jul08.pdf.

Rhim, L. M., J. Faukner, and M. J. McLaughlin. 2006. *Project Intersect research report #5: Access and accountability for students with disabilities in California charter schools.* College Park, MD: University of Maryland, Project Intersect.

Rhim, L. M., C. M. Lange, E. A. Ahearn, and M. J. McLaughlin. 2005. *Project Intersect research report #3: Survey of state charter school officials.* College Park, MD: University of Maryland, Project Intersect.

-------. 2006. *Project Intersect research report #4: Charter school special education infrastructures.* College Park, MD: University of Maryland, Project Intersect.

-------. 2007a. *Project Intersect research report #7: Survey of charter school operators.* College Park, MD: University of Maryland, Project Intersect.

-------. 2007b. *Project Intersect research report #6: Survey of charter school authorizers.* College Park, MD: University of Maryland, Project Intersect.

Rhim, L. M., and M. J. McLaughlin. 2007a. Accountability frameworks and students with disabilities: A test of assumptions about improving public education for all students. *International Journal of Disability, Development and Education,* 54(1).

-------. 2007b. Students with disabilities in charter schools: What we now know. *Focus on Exceptional Children* 39(5).

Shields, R. 2005. *Texas charter schools and students with disabilities: Parental perceptions of the phenomenon.* Unpublished doctoral dissertation, University of Texas.

Simon, H. 1976. *Administrative behavior* (3d ed.). New York: Free Press.

Skrtic, T. 1991. The special education paradox: Equity as the way to excellence. *Harvard Educational Review* 61.2: 148–206.

Sullins, C., and G. Miron. 2005. *Challenges of starting and operating charter schools: A multicase study.* Kalamazoo, MI: The Evaluation Center. Available at http://www.wmich.edu/evalctr/charter/cs_challenges_report.pdf

Summers, J., L. Hoffman, J. Marquis, A. Turnbull, and D. Poston. 2005. Relationship between parent satisfaction regarding partnerships with professionals and age of child. *Topics in Early Childhood Special Education,* 25(1): 48-58.

Swanson, E. 2004. Special education services in charter schools. *The Educational Forum,* 69(1): 34-43, Fall 2004.

Szabo, J. M., and M. M. Gerber. 1996. Special education and the charter school movement. *Special Education Leadership Review*, 3: 135-148.

Tamber, C. July 31, 2007. Charter schools win funding case in Md. Court of Appeals. *The (Baltimore) Daily Record*.

Teske, P., J. Fitzpatrick, and G. Kaplan. 2007. *Opening doors: How low-income parents search for the right school*. Seattle: Center on Reinventing Public Education.

Teske, P., and R. Reichardt. 2006. Doing their homework: How charter school parents make their choices. In *Hopes, fears, & reality: A balanced look at American charter schools in 2006*, ed. R. Lake and P. Hill. National Charter School Research Project. Seattle: Center on Reinventing Public Education.

Thomas B. Fordham Institute. 2005. *Charter school funding: Inequities new frontier*. Washington, DC. Available at: http://www.edexcellence.net:80/institute/charterfinance/.

U.S. Department of Education. 2005. *The 27th Annual report to Congress on the implementation of the Individuals with Disabilities Education Act*. Available at http://www.ed.gov/about/reports/annual/osep/2005/parts-b-c/index.html.

U.S. Department of Education, National Center for Education Statistics. 2008. *Digest of Education Statistics 2007. (NCES 2008-022)*.

U.S. Department of Education, National Center for Education Statistics, Common Core of Data. 2007. *Public elementary/secondary school universe survey, 2005–06, version 1a*. Available at http://nces.ed.gov/pubs2007/pesschools06/tables/table_5.asp.

U. S. Department of Education, Office of Innovation and Improvement. 2007. *K–8 charter schools: Closing the achievement gap*.

U.S. Department of Education, Office of Special Education and Rehabilitative Services, Office of Special Education Programs. 2009. *28th Annual Report to Congress on the Implementation of the Individuals with Disabilities Education Act, 2006*, vol. 1. Washington, DC. Available at http://www2.ed.gov/about/reports/annual/osep/2006/parts-b-c/28th-vol-1.pdf.

U.S. Department of Education, Office of Special Education Programs, Data Analysis System (DANS). 2006. *OMB #1820-0043: Table 1-17, "Children with Disabilities Receiving Special Education Under Part B of the Individuals with Disabilities Education Act," 2006*. Downloaded February 26, 2010 from https://www.ideadata.org/arc_toc8.asp#partbCC.

Wells, A. S., S. Artiles, C. W. Carnochan, C. Cooper, J. J. Grutzik, and A. Holme. 1998. *Beyond the rhetoric of charter school reform: A study of ten California school districts*. Los Angeles: University of California at Los Angeles Graduate School of Education and Information.

Wisconsin Department of Public Instruction. 2008. *Wisconsin charter school yearbook*. Madison, WI.

Woodland Elementary Charter School, Renewal application, 2006: 74. Available at http://www.fultonschools.org/school/woodlandes/main/Our_Charter.pdf.

Ziebarth, T. 2007. *Charter school dashboard 2007*. Washington DC: National Alliance for Public Charter Schools.

Contributors

DANA BRINSON is a consultant with Public Impact, an education policy and management consulting firm. She has conducted research and analysis on a wide variety of education issues, including education philanthropy, school improvement and turnarounds, disconnected youth, and charter schools. She holds a B.A. from West Virginia University in Psychology and History, and an M.A. from the University of North Carolina-Chapel Hill in European and Women's History. She is a former history teacher and special educator.

KELLY HUPFELD is the Assistant Dean for Special Projects at the School of Public Affairs, University of Colorado Denver. She is also a Research Assistant Professor with the Center for Education Policy Analysis, housed in the School of Public Affairs. She received her law degree from Northwestern University School of Law in 1991, and practiced law for seven years prior to moving into the public policy arena. Areas of interest include school leadership, school choice, teacher quality, and education systems. She is the mother of two children attending charter schools in the Denver area, one of whom receives special education services.

JOANNE JACOBS is formerly a Knight-Ridder op-ed columnist and *San Jose Mercury News* editorial writer. She started an education blog at joannejacobs.com in 2001, and is the author of *Our School: The Inspiring Story of Two Teachers, One Big Idea, and the Charter School That Beat the Odds* (Palgrave Macmillan, 2005).

ROBIN J. LAKE is Associate Director of the Center on Reinventing Public Education, where she specializes in charter school research and policy development that focuses on effective accountability policies, scale and supply, and school district use of chartering as a reform strategy. Ms. Lake is also Executive Director of the Center's National Charter School Research Project (NCSRP), which was established in late 2004 by a consortium of funders in an effort to improve the balance, rigor, and application of charter school research. Lake has authored numerous studies and technical assistance reports on charter schools. She is co-author, with Paul Hill, of *Charter Schools and Accountability in Public Education* (Brookings Press) and editor of the annual report, *Hopes, Fears, & Reality: A Balanced Look at American Charter Schools*. Ms. Lake holds a B.A. in International Studies and an M.A. in Public Administration from the University of Washington.

TRACEY O'BRIEN is a Senior Research Associate with the Center for Education Policy Analysis in the School of Public Affairs, University of Colorado Denver. She received her M.A. in Public Administration from the University of Colorado Denver in 1993. Ms. O'Brien conducts research and program evaluation, and she provides data management training and technical assistance. Areas of interest include school choice, PreK–12 education, parent involvement, poverty, and homelessness.

LAUREN MORANDO RHIM is a consultant specializing in critical education issues, including school transformation, special education, state and district support for school improvement, charter schools, and virtual schools. Rhim conducted this research in her prior position as a senior consultant with Public Impact, an education policy and management consulting firm. She holds a Ph.D. in Social Foundations of Education Policy and Leadership from the University of Maryland, College Park.

PAUL TESKE is Dean of the School of Public Affairs at the University of Colorado Denver, and University of Colorado Distinguished Professor. He has co-authored a book on school choice (*Choosing Schools*, Princeton University Press, 2000, with Mark Schneider and Melissa Marschall) and several other studies of how urban parents make school choices. His most recent education book is *Pay-for-Performance Teacher Compensation* (Harvard Education Press, 2007, with Phil Gonring and Brad Jupp).

Made in the USA
Charleston, SC
26 April 2010